GODS, GUIDES AND GUARDIAN ANGELS

by international best-selling author and psychic

Richard Lawrence
with Mark Bennett

Winchester, UK
Washington, USA

First published by O Books, 2007
O Books is an imprint of John Hunt Publishing Ltd.,
The Bothy, Deershot Lodge, Park Lane, Ropley, Hants, SO24 0BE, UK
office1@o-books.net
www.o-books.net

Distribution in:

UK and Europe
Orca Book Services
orders@orcabookservices.co.uk
Tel: 01202 665432 Fax: 01202 666219 Int. code (44)

USA and Canada
NBN
custserv@nbnbooks.com
Tel: 1 800 462 6420 Fax: 1 800 338 4550

Australia and New Zealand
Brumby Books
sales@brumbybooks.com.au
Tel: 61 3 9761 5535 Fax: 61 3 9761 7095

Far East (offices in Singapore, Thailand, Hong Kong, Taiwan)
Pansing Distribution Pte Ltd
kemal@pansing.com
Tel: 65 6319 9939 Fax: 65 6462 5761

South Africa
Alternative Books
altbook@peterhyde.co.za
Tel: 021 447 5300 Fax: 021 447 1430

Text copyright Richard Lawrence 2007

Design: Stuart Davies
Author photograph by Fabrice Rizzato

ISBN-13: 978 1 84694 051 4

A CIP catalogue record for this book is available from the British Library.

Printed in the US by Maple Vail

GODS, GUIDES AND GUARDIAN ANGELS

by international best-selling author and psychic

Richard Lawrence

with Mark Bennett

BOOKS

Winchester, UK
Washington, USA

Other titles by Richard Lawrence include

Unlock Your Psychic Powers
Contacts with the Gods from Space (co-authored with
Dr George King)
Realise Your Inner Potential (co-authored with
Dr George King)
The Meditation Plan
Little Book of Karma
The Magic of Healing
Meditation: a complete workout for the mind

ACKNOWLEDGEMENTS

I owe an immense debt to my co-author Mark Bennett, who has taken my original material and been largely responsible for producing the book in its present form. He also did extensive additional research for which I am very grateful.

I am also grateful to Noémi Perkin for assisting Mark with his additional research and to her and Nikki Perrott for transcribing the many hours of my tapes which formed the basis of the book.

I am indebted to all my fellow International Directors of The Aetherius Society, for which I work, for supporting this project from the beginning. I am particularly grateful to Dr John Holder, Steve Gibson, Pat Higginson and Lesley Young for their input and improvements to the original manuscript.

I must thank Fiona Spencer Thomas, my literary agent, for her enthusiasm from the outset and John Hunt, my publisher, for having a completely open mind towards it.

Above all, I would like to thank my wife, Alyson, who has always believed in my psychic and channelling experiences since I started over twenty-five years ago. Without her love and support for my work throughout the years, I would not be in a position to write this book today.

Richard Lawrence

CONTENTS

FOREWORD

"In heaven an angel is nobody in particular"
George Bernard Shaw

She was a petite brunette wearing a dark blue 1940s-style skirt. She looked radiant – so radiant in fact that I could clearly see white light shining all around her. This, coupled with her gentle smile made her look so happy, so full of life – there's simply no other way to put it. That's the ironic thing about it: she'd been dead for more than three decades and yet she looked so full of life. It sounds strange, I know, but it's a fact that no one looks more alive than when they're dead.

She was called *Pixie*.

* * *

It was late afternoon one perfect summer's day in early 1980, though to an Englishman virtually every day in Australia seems like summer. The sky was that kind of intense shade of blue you don't seem to get in the northern hemisphere, and the heat was all-embracing yet strangely unoppressive.

Perth is one of the most beautiful cities I have ever been to – a harmonious blend of old and new, busy and quiet, leafy and cosmopolitan – and I enjoyed the short walk from where I was staying to the house of... let's call her Mrs Smith.

I was on a lecture tour and Mrs Smith was a friend of the man who had kindly agreed to be my driver. She had expressed a serious interest in The Aetherius Society, the spiritual organisation I was working for (and still do work for – over a quarter of a century later).

That's why I was going to meet her – to answer her metaphysical questions.

She lived in a large, attractive, terraced house in a pleasant middle-class suburb. I rang the bell. She invited me in through a smart hallway to a well-furnished sitting-room, where we sat down and started chatting about all kinds of spiritual matters of interest to us both.

Between sips of tea, and the munching of biscuits, I became aware of the image of a young woman. It was blurred at first, but became steadily clearer, more defined; it was a little like looking through binoculars which are being adjusted to the right setting. At first I thought it must be my imagination, as you would, but pictures in the imagination flicker and fade, whereas this became stronger and stronger.

My eyes were open. I could see her standing on my left. She looked as real as when you look at anyone else – there was nothing "ghostly" about her. She wasn't see-through like a hologram. But nevertheless somehow I knew that I was looking at her clairvoyantly; that my ability to see her was dependent upon my state of mind.

Then a name came to me. She didn't say it out loud. It just came to me.

I don't remember the exact words, but the conversation with Mrs Smith went something like this:

"I'm sorry, but does the name 'Pixie' mean anything to you?" I asked.

Mrs Smith looked at me, shocked.

"Well yes, actually it does, she was my best friend, whatever made you ask that?!"

"She's here." I replied calmly.

"What do you mean? She's been dead for years!" She retorted, with a tinge of sadness in her voice.

"Yes, I know. She's wearing old-fashioned clothes – a dark-blue skirt – forties-style. She's got a message for you."

Her expression brightened as she realised what was happening.

"What… from the 'other side', you mean? Well… Goodness me! This is amazing! Forties you say… yes, that would make sense, she died during the war, you see… how is she?"

"She's fine. She wants you to know she still cares for you – and she looks out for you."

"Like a guardian angel?"

"Yes."

Pixie told me a few more things, which I duly related to Mrs Smith, who was deeply moved and extremely impressed at my mediumistic abilities.

The only problem was: I wasn't a medium.

I walked out of the house totally stunned by what had seemed so normal and natural at the time. Actually the fact that it had seemed so normal and natural at the time made it seem all the more unbelievable and strange to me afterwards. I was virtually pinching myself in disbelief, expecting to wake up at any moment.

It wasn't that I was a sceptic of this kind of thing – on the contrary, I *believed* in it very much. I just didn't know that I could *do* it.

It never occurs to a toddler when they're excitedly taking their first steps that one day they'll be able to run a mile.

CHAPTER 1

Transition

"For in that sleep of death what dreams may come
When we have shuffled off this mortal coil"
William Shakespeare

Some people think it is impossible to know what happens to us after death. They are wrong.

Half Moon Hill
The Plains of Saint Theodore
1st March 2003

Dear Ricardo,
The weather here is perfect – blue sky, just a little shower now and then. Animals aplenty – lambs and dogs mainly. No one lives here exactly but many visit; they float in, as it were, from many other locations just as I have done for this rendezvous. It is a most pleasant "zone", if you like, most suitable for communications such as this one.
Love and affectionate greetings as ever,

Nicholas

A few years ago one of my closest friends passed away. He was only in his late forties and, even though he'd been ill for a few months, it came as a terrible shock to me.

He was an unusual man. You don't find many people like him any more. A timeless English gentleman of the old school. He was an Oxford graduate with a degree in English Literature, and maintained a strong interest in British history and poetry throughout his life – often quoting Shakespeare over lunch, or Wordsworth over tea, never hesitating or making a single error. In conversation it was easy to mistake him for someone from an entirely different generation. I remember listening with rapt attention as he keenly discussed with my parents incidents much closer to their lives than to mine, like the D-Day landings or the abdication of Edward VIII, even though we were almost the same age and these things had happened long before we were born. But his erudition and traditional manners were no barrier to his ability to entertain, make friends and socialise. He was always good company – beneath a serious exterior lurked a mischievous wit which never stayed hidden for long.

One day a few weeks after his passing, I was sitting in my drawing-room (as he would have called it) when I became aware of a presence. I had over twenty years of experience under my belt since the *Pixie* incident, and my concentration was no longer marred by doubt or surprise. I knew what was happening. I knew what to do. I knew it was friendly.

And I knew it was Nicholas.

I got up and sat down with pen and paper – ready. Word by word, phrase by phrase, I was dictated a letter from the "other side". It was the first time I had ever received a message in letter format. How like him! Ever a fan of correct protocol, Nicholas hadn't chosen to just casually tell me a few things like most people would: he'd chosen to do it *properly*. Above is a short excerpt from the first of four such communications, which give a glimpse into what life is really like beyond death – a question which had always interested him while he was alive. In fact, he'd always bemoaned the fact that mediums didn't have more to say on this important subject.

His second letter, again addressed to "Ricardo", his nickname for me, reads as follows:

Spoon Jetty
The Lake of Sorrow
27th March 2003

Dear Ricardo,
Life here is an unravelling adventure as though time is more densely filled with experience of different kinds. Change is quickened here by learning faster from simple things: the dance of a tiny fawn in the thicket, the stern hectoring of a dull theologian, the new light in my life - my mentor whom I call She Who Must Be Obeyed.
We eat occasionally, we drink even less, including fine wine which I can now sample. We never smoke, though we do taste tobacco and other plants. I am learning to write, paint a little and play something akin to a harmonium. Sometimes when I feel wretched I can see, over a distance of countless miles, theatrical productions from different realms including *Othello* and others, when I am permitted to do so. I have also seen a new cinematic production called *Sands of Borrowed Time*.
Tomorrow I shall depart this location for new pastures - literally and metaphorically - and soon I will have a glimpse of my guru. I do miss the small things so very much, but they tell me here that all things pass on and so must we.

My felicitations to all,

Nicholas

Actually Nicholas isn't his real name. I've changed his name, and edited out some private details from his letters, so as to in no way bring unnecessary upset to those who were close to him.

This letter shows life after death to be not so very different from life before death – eating, drinking, learning, watching plays, etc. He's not sitting around on a cloud, nor does he show any sign of having sprouted wings. This theme is also to be found in *The Egyptian Book of the Dead*, which as well as mentioning eating and drinking, also includes ploughing and reaping among the activities which go on, and talks of cities.

People do often change after death, but they don't normally change that much. Priorities may shift, usually in a more spiritual direction – it is rare to hear of any genuine medium receiving a message about interest rates, soap operas, or the world cup, whereas it is common for discarnates (people who have passed on) to say that they feel much more at peace after death. And many who die do indeed become "guardian angels", in the sense that they watch over people who are still alive. However, just because you die, doesn't mean you become a saint or an all-knowing sage – nor does it mean that you enjoy the fruits of eternal bliss in a starry, nebulous heaven chatting to God whenever you wish to.

For me it was a revelation to discover the truth about life after death, which I did from the teachings of my guru, the great yoga Master and medium Dr George King, founder of The Aetherius Society. It is his knowledge and wisdom which have been the bedrock of my understanding of this subject, enhanced by my own personal experiences, which have confirmed what he taught me.

Orthodox ideas of heaven and hell had always baffled me. Have you ever met anyone who would really be suited to eternal "heaven"? How many people do you know who would even really like it? Grapes aren't most people's favourite food, and playing the harp isn't most people's favourite hobby. And just because someone is dead, it doesn't mean they are going to want to start hanging out with choirs of angels singing in exultation and doing little else. I don't know anyone who could stick it for a year let alone eternity!

And what about hell? Fiery lakes of boiling sulphur? Being prodded with pitchforks by nightmarish monsters like something out of a painting by Hieronymus Bosch? Have you ever met anyone so bad that they might deserve an eternity of pure suffering? I wouldn't wish that on my worst enemy – so the idea that a benevolent God could do that to someone just for not believing in him is bizarre. The notion of an eternity of anything, especially of hell with no hope of redemption, sounds to me more like the twisted dream of an embittered tyrant, than the perfect justice of a loving Deity.

When it comes to thinking about life after death, generally people are not logical; in fact they turn away from logic with disdain, as though it is a useless, worldly hindrance to an understanding of the life hereafter. This, in my opinion, is a great shame.

Atheistic scientists who evangelise about the mortality of the human lot, claiming with an irrational certainty that all consciousness ceases when the heart stops beating, are missing something. Not only have they managed to completely repress the voice of intuition within them, which affirms that life does indeed continue after death; not only are they choosing to ignore the voluminous evidence supporting the idea of life after death – and communication with the deceased; but they are also ignoring basic logic.

Why should consciousness cease after the death of the physical body? Science doesn't even fully understand what consciousness is, so how can any scientist claim to know what happens to it? Things don't just vanish, or go through an unrecognisable degree of change for no reason. And death of the physical body is no reason for consciousness to vanish or go through an unrecognisable degree of change: consciousness does not require a physical body – a fact backed up by research.

And what does consciousness do? It experiences life. And in so doing it gains understanding of life. Different people need, and deserve, different experiences. A selfless humanitarian, who has sacrificed the peace and tranquillity of a mountain monastery in order to help the starving masses, deserves to experience great spiritual joy and peace. A vicious murderer, on the other hand, needs to understand the pain his actions have caused others – for his own sake rather than for the sake of his victims. This is a natural law, every bit as logical, and impersonal, as gravity. It is a law far removed from our feeble concept of law – a law which is completely fair, and absolutely exact. It is called the Law of *Karma*. In Buddhism this is equated to the Newton's third law of motion which states that every action has an equal and opposite *re*action. In Christianity it is simply described as the fact that: "…whatsoever a man soweth, that shall he also reap." (Galatians 6.7). So-called "negative" karma is not there to punish, but to teach, as indeed is "positive" karma.

Metaphysicians have for thousands of years talked of other

planes of existence attached to this earth – integral to the earth, but operating on different frequencies of vibration. This is similar to the concept of "*lokas*" in Hindu philosophy. Unless you are clairvoyant, you can't see these "planes", or "realms", while you are alive, but when you pass on, this is where you go. And when you are there, the realm you are on will seem every bit as real to you as this realm seems to you now. Although we may talk about "leaving the 'physical' body when we die", what we really mean is that we are leaving one kind of physicality for another, because all these realms are physical, it's just that they are physical at different frequencies.

There are six realms which are "higher" than the one we're on now (level one), and four realms which are "lower" ("high" and "low" in terms of frequency of vibration). This is where the simplistic orthodox idea of heaven and hell comes from. The "higher" vibratory levels are "heavens", the "lower" ones are "hells" – though some of the other realms are in many ways not all that different from certain places on this realm.

Note that it is not the whim of an autocratic overlord which determines which realm we go to. The choice is ours. It is our own consciousness, our own need for experience, based on our past thought and action – it is, in a word, our *karma*.

We go to where we best fit in, to the realm which vibrates on a similar level to our own consciousness, to the place where we can best learn the lessons we need to learn. So the vicious murderer will go "down" to a lower realm, and the self-sacrificing humanitarian will go "up" to a higher realm. If someone were to be on the wrong realm, even if it was a higher realm, it could be quite cruel, even just on an emotional level – never mind from an evolutionary point of view – because so much of what was familiar to them would be absent. It would be like taking an average family man from London and putting him in a Buddhist monastery in Bhutan. The transition from this realm can be hard enough as it is, even without people ending up where they don't belong, as we can see in these letters.

While receiving Nicholas's next letter, I could not only feel his presence, but I could see him, clairvoyantly, as a strong mental image, looking very much alive – a world away from the stereotypical idea of a grim, pale, translucent spectre. He was wearing a smart dark blue jacket buttoned across, almost like a uniform, with a round collar. He seemed altogether better.

The House by the Waterside
17th May 2003

Dear Ricardo,
This will be my last letter to you in this form, because I know how busy you are and I too have other new-found duties. I am learning so much so fast that it boggles the mind, but it certainly inspires you on to higher things. This is my new home and I love it. From here I travel wheresoever I choose, within reason. Certain times are set aside for learning through study, or from a particular teacher of which there are several in this region...
[...]
Now to my friend and teacher. His name is Baba [*which means "father" and is a common name for a guru*] to those of us who hang on his every word. He is a mine of knowledge, wisdom, insights and useful nuggets of information. He is exactly what I have been searching for. I also receive counsel, albeit

uncompromising and stern as it often is, from She Who Must Be Obeyed. I will not reveal her identity because she does not permit it. But overall I am happy, settled and know exactly what I have to do.

God bless you dear Richard – my love as ever,

Nicholas

What a difference! In the previous letter he is OK, but clearly having a few problems adjusting, whereas here he is unambiguously upbeat.

We begin to see a gradual progression, as Nicholas settles in and gets used to his new life. Had he had a clearer sense of what life after death was really like, and of his own karmic pattern, even if only in the last few days of his life, I have little doubt that he would have found his transition easier. I believe that She Who Must Be Obeyed, mentioned above, is in fact someone who helped Nicholas during his transition. She could either be one of those who specialise in helping people to settle in to their new realm, or it could be that she chose to help him because she had a particular interest in him, or connection with him.

He was a spiritual person, who understood yoga philosophy, so imagine what problems a complete non-believer who dies suddenly may have. I hope very much that this book, in giving readers a greater appreciation of life after death, may help people, when the time comes, to move on in a natural, gentle way that is less hampered by the fear and confusion which confronts so many in our secular age at this crucial time. Generally a deceased person will go to a "realm of waiting" for a period of time before settling in their new abode. Nicholas's letters gave me new insights into how this process of transition can take place.

In addition to it being extremely helpful for the transitioner to have an understanding of what life after death is really like, it is also possible for someone to smooth their own transition from this realm to the next by spending the last moments of their life mentally preparing themselves for what is to come. The idea that what happens to a person just prior to death can affect what happens afterwards is reflected – albeit in very different ways – in various cultures around the world.

In the Hindu classic, the *Bhagavad Gita*, Sri Krishna tells Arjuna that one achieves that state of being which is in one's mind as one leaves the body. In China, there was a practice of shaving the head of someone on the brink of death, trimming their nails, and seating them upright. This was regarded as having a positive influence on the soul's departure from the body.

In the Buddhist *Bardo Thödol*, or *The Tibetan Book of the Dead*, as it is commonly known in the West, there is detailed instruction on how to treat the dying. A guru reads over and over again a certain short piece of text from the book in the ear of the person dying, then, when the person is literally on the brink of death, they are turned onto their right side, the arteries on both sides of their throat are pressed, and they are prevented from sleeping, since it is regarded as vital that they be awake in order to be fully aware of the transition as it occurs. More reading follows, advising the transitioner on what is going on, and how their mind should be focused. It is thought it takes three and a half to four days for the transitioner to completely detach from their physical body. It is possible for a priest known as a *hpho-bo* (pronounced *pho-o*) to shorten this period, but even so, the transitioner will not realise that this detachment has taken place until the three and a half to four days are up.

In Roman Catholicism we find the practice of the "anointing of the sick", formerly known as "extreme unction", or "the last rites", which is when someone who is terminally ill confesses to a priest, is given absolution and is then anointed with consecrated oil just prior to death. For Medieval Christians those last few breaths were especially important, since they believed that there were demons lurking nearby, waiting to grab an emerging soul at the point of transition.

I wouldn't practise any of these near-death rituals myself, but nevertheless I believe that they are more than just tradition or superstition: they appear to be indicative of a latent appreciation of how important it is to pass on with a degree of awareness of what is to come.

In Nicholas's last missive, which wasn't given in a normal letter format, perhaps indicating his detachment from the conventions of this realm, he not only seems happy where he is, but even goes as far as to be critical of our realm. I felt this marked the completion of his transition to the realm he was meant to settle on.

6th January 2004

I am now domiciled in a community of European and Himalayan peoples all of whom share a consuming passion for spiritual wisdom, including myself. I have had to become multilingual which is far and away an easier proposition in this realm of thought than it would be on your turgid plane where people move so interminably slowly. Long-distance communication is

very easy here, especially at certain times such as early evening
and early morning.

Here we get a glimpse of the fact that the after-death realms are
much "finer", or "subtler", than this one. Things tend to happen
faster and more easily. This is because thought has much more
power on the other realms than on this one. Magic is a much less
fantastical concept. Life, on the higher realms at least, is much less
limited than it is here. In fact, not only do most people *look* more
alive after they die, but they also *feel* more alive.

But this physical realm is still the most important to be on. Here
everyone is thrown together – in the same century both Hitler and
Mother Teresa inhabited the physical realm. Although this realm is
more "turgid", as Nicholas puts it – in fact *because* it is more
turgid – this is where the greatest challenges lie, in terms of
personal development and helping others, and, consequently this is
the realm where, as a general rule you can make the most difference.
So, just as the need for experience pulls us from this world to the
next, it also takes us back again from the next world to this one. Just
prior to birth, our soul chooses the environment and parents we are
to be born to in order to gain the experiences we need and deserve.
This is a complex matter. It is certainly not a case that all good
people are born to wonderful parents, or that all bad people are born
into terrible poverty. Someone with a lot of very good karma, may
choose to be born into a difficult situation in order to learn some
tough lessons very quickly, whereas a much less evolved person may
be born to great luxury because they have somehow earned this
opportunity, but the lesson they actually need to learn is detachment
from materialism.

And so we pass from life to life, spending some time on the after-death realms between lives, always learning, and, if we make the right decisions, always progressing. How quickly we progress depends on us – depends on how much effort we put into learning the Divine Laws and putting them into action throughout our lives. Eventually, when all the lessons we need to learn have been fully learnt, we escape reincarnation and move on to higher things.

CHAPTER 2

Channelling

"The voice of the dead was a living voice to me"
Alfred, Lord Tennyson

I wasn't born psychic. I was perfectly ordinary as a child, which was in some ways fortunate for me, as many psychic children find it very hard growing up in an unpsychic world – met by confusion, condescension, and sometimes downright lies at every turn, as well-meaning adults try to do the "right thing" in helping them to snap out of their "fantasies".

It wasn't until I had found The Aetherius Society, and practised the techniques taught by Dr George King, for a few years, that my psychic abilities began to awaken. That's why I know that everyone can develop psychic abilities in one way or another.

Back in 1976, when I was only 23, I used to give spiritual healing at The Aetherius Society's Healing Sanctuary in London. One day a patient who was a well-known medium came for a healing treatment. In fact, she was so highly skilled that she could sit down at a piano and play excellent, improvised music by channelling a musician – when she herself had very limited musical ability. As soon as you saw her it was clear that she was a successful, well-known person – a smartly dressed woman in her early sixties, accompanied by a man of similar age.

I greeted her and we sat down. Before I had a chance to start talking to her about the healing treatment she was about to receive, she began to tell me that she could see a guide behind me, in a white coat (Aetherius Society healers wear white coats), which I found interesting, but not especially remarkable – she was a medium after all and that's the kind of thing mediums do. But she went on to say that he was telling her that I would one day have the ability that she had. This baffled me a bit, since I was no more psychic than anyone else at that time. The idea that in time I would be able to communicate with discarnates seemed hopelessly improbable. But then she told me who the guide was: Sir Oliver Lodge – a name I recognised instantly as the great scientist who devoted much of his life to researching the scientific validity of life after death, and, more significantly, as far as I was concerned, a man who had spoken through Dr King in the early years of The Aetherius Society, unbeknown to this lady.

A couple of years later I met a prominent metaphysician called Dr George Hall, who was a member of the advisory council of the Festival of Mind & Body when the word "Spirit" was added – a change he was very keen on – and indeed the phrase "Mind Body Spirit" is of course still with us as an umbrella term for all alternative spirituality today. He was an advanced person, who had lived for a time in the ashram of the wonderful Indian yogi Paramahansa Yogananda. He definitely had spiritual abilities: even when he was quite elderly, he used to get up at 4am every morning to commune with intelligences he referred to as belonging to "The Great White Lodge". He was genuinely impressive. He lived and breathed spirituality. He would talk metaphysics incessantly – as soon as pleasantries had been exchanged he'd be away, not wishing to waste a single second of an opportunity to talk about the work which was his passion. And unlike most people who talk incessantly, he talked with authority and depth about a wide range of very interesting subjects.

Almost as distinctive in appearance as he was in character, he walked with a large wooden stick with a rounded silver top, and wore a large amethyst ring. His visits always caused great interest at Aetherius House, the Headquarters of The Aetherius Society in London, and not without good reason – you never knew what fascinating nugget of information he might come out with. On one occasion, with complete confidence, he casually mentioned to me that higher entities wanted to communicate with me, but that I wasn't yet ready because I still had too much ego! A just criticism, I have no doubt.

Not long after that I did indeed begin to get messages from the departed. Once it stopped being so strange, and I got over the "how can this be when I'm not a medium" mindset, I began to really enjoy it. It was satisfying – and very exhilarating. And it didn't just plateau out; I kept learning and improving.

Sometimes when I was driving in an area I didn't know too well, I would get training in clairaudience (psychic hearing) from a guide. He would say something like: "Turn left, and third on the right will be a fish and chip shop." If this turned out to be true, I knew I really had been listening to the guide, if it didn't, I knew it was my imagination, or lack of concentration in hearing the message correctly. This was a great help to me in the first few years of my development. Though I must stress that learning psychic abilities while driving a car is not to be recommended as a safe practice!

One of the people who supported me most in those early days was Dr King's wife, Dr Monique King. I gave her many readings and she gave me great encouragement, including helping me to get the right kind of crystal ball – my chosen "tool". It attracted me in a kind of Taoist way, because of its wholeness, as suggested by its spherical shape, and also because of its emptiness – a void from which insights would be drawn.

Dr King himself didn't find out that I was giving readings until one apparently chance happening in a restaurant in New York. I wasn't trying to keep it secret from him, I just didn't want to bother him with it; being psychic may seem amazing to the average person, but to a Master the calibre of Dr King I felt that my psychic abilities would seem quite insignificant.

There were three of us: Dr King, myself and another of Dr King's students, my good friend Ray Nielsen. We had been looking for somewhere to eat for a while, and all we could find was a very crowded diner. They had run out of tables for three, so Dr King and Ray sat at one table, and I sat at another opposite a woman I didn't know. Shortly after I had started my meal she began to cry. I asked her what the matter was, and she began talking about various problems in her personal life. I tuned in and was able to give her some psychic guidance. She was so impressed and grateful that when the three of us came to leave, she told Dr King and Ray what a wonderful reading she'd had and how helpful I had been to her. Dr King was a little surprised, and told me off for not having told him about the fact that I had been giving readings. But from then on he was wonderfully supportive – and even designed my crystal ball cover, making sure it had the right astrological symbols on it. He advised me to give readings regularly saying, "If you don't use it, you'll lose it." So I became a professional psychic consultant, donating all fees to the work of The Aetherius Society.

He taught in unusual ways, and I'm sure he helped me more than I fully understand. He didn't give me any instruction *per se*, instead he would just give occasional pointers, often more significant than they first appeared. For example, he told me once that the more I talked, the more would come to me. On the face of it, banal advice, but it turned out to be completely true.

You may be wondering how you know you're not just imagining things when you start getting psychic impressions. The simplest, and most basic, answer to that is that a great deal of the information a psychic or medium receives should be verifiable, and a great deal of the information I was getting was indeed verified by the people I was giving readings to. When *Pixie* contacted me, I was able to tell the lady I was with details which I could not have known from anywhere but the lady herself – details accurate enough to be beyond guessability; getting the name "Pixie" itself is a world away from saying to an audience of 50 people: "Does anyone know a 'John'?"

Of course I could be making the whole story up: that's a question for your own intuition and rational assessment – I can't prove any of these things to you from these pages. All I can do is relate the facts as accurately as I recall in the hope that this book might get people thinking and help them better understand what being psychic is all about. Even if I could prove every one of my experiences to you, would it really make that much difference to your life? Quite possibly not. What would make a difference to your life, however, is if this book inspired you to gain the ability to prove this type of thing to yourself, by developing your own latent psychic and intuitive powers through spiritual techniques such as the ones I learnt from Dr King. Then, and only then, would you really know for sure that psychic ability really does exist.

Assuming then that communication with other realms is indeed possible, how does it happen? Is there more than one way for information to be received?

Yes. Three of the most important are: trance; psychically hearing words; and psychically picking up thoughts.

Trance is where you enter a state in which you are not fully conscious and an entity speaks through you, using your voice box. So if you hear a medium in trance, they will actually, to some degree at least, sound like the communicating entity. There are basically two types of trance: positive and negative. The positive mediumistic trance state is extremely rare indeed and it takes a very advanced person to be able to achieve it. Dr King frequently entered a positive trance in order to let higher intelligences speak through him. He would do this by first inducing a deep meditative state which only an extremely accomplished adept in a spiritual discipline, such as the higher forms of yoga, could achieve. He moved from a conscious state to a superconscious state, and, in doing so, always had complete control over the trance condition adopted. (See Chapters 10 and 12 for more information on higher states of consciousness and Dr King's mediumship respectively)

The negative trance state is much easier and much more common. I'm glad to say, however, that it seems to have been losing popularity over recent years. Mediums were trained, usually in "development circles", to blank their minds, thereby entering a passive state, which meant that an entity from another realm could come and take them over for a period of time. Sometimes the entity would go as far as to enter their aura, which is even more invasive. Afterwards the medium has little or no knowledge of the content of the message, because they were not sufficiently conscious while it was coming through. This kind of trance can be dangerous in that the medium has virtually no control over what entity speaks through them. It is also quite debilitating, in that, in a subtle way, allowing another entity to speak through you weakens your own will – it's as though every time you do it you lose a part of yourself. I have never fully entered a negative trance, but I did for a short time try a light, partial trance condition and discovered for myself a loss of will-power in my everyday life. I should have known better than to try this, but it did teach me an important lesson.

Some people use illegal drugs or alcohol to induce this kind of state. This is unwise to say the least. Drugs in particular are to be avoided at all costs in this kind of work, not because they don't work, but because they do – in a way that is extremely difficult to control. Not only this, but drugs affect the aura, often causing considerable damage. A person who has a drug-induced "spiritual" or psychic experience, while the experience may well have been genuine, is moving down the ladder of evolution rather than up it. Life is about mastery of experience – not experience for experience's sake, and drugs will reduce the control you have over your experience – psychically, spiritually, and throughout your life. (Note: I am not talking about taking essential drugs for medical reasons, or about having a glass of wine with your dinner, I am talking about drug and alcohol abuse.)

A person who practises negative trance could even find themselves entering such a trance and being taken over by a malevolent discarnate during their everyday life – while eating, driving, or doing their shopping. I would not recommend this kind of trance state to anyone: the potential benefits are vastly outweighed by the dangers.

Psychically receiving thoughts is probably the most common

way that mediums today communicate with the spirit world, whereas hearing words psychically is much more difficult. In the *Pixie* story I was picking up thoughts, whereas when I channel messages now, I often hear each word individually, which requires intense concentration and a conscious suspension of my own thought.

Many psychics will combine receiving thoughts and hearing words, without being particularly aware which they are doing at any given time. They will also use their intuition: that inner voice which speaks only truth, provided your mind is quiet enough to hear it. In some ways it doesn't matter which method is used as long as the messages received are accurate and helpful.

You get some psychics who believe they are listening to a guide, when in fact they are listening to their own intuition, and others who believe they are listening to their intuition, when in fact it is a guide – and many psychics who do a bit of both, and aren't quite sure which they are doing at any one time. This can happen to people who don't consider themselves psychic as well. I once talked to a Royal Air Force serviceman who told me that on one occasion he had been about to parachute out of a plane when he "heard a voice" telling him to check his parachute. He knew it had already been checked, but he checked it again anyway and found that it hadn't been packed properly; if he hadn't checked again he would almost certainly have died. Whether the "voice" was a guardian angel or his intuition remained a mystery to him.

I certainly don't always know where all my impressions come from, often there isn't time to concentrate sufficiently to identify the source. But spiritual and psychic development is all about mental control, and if you are to ever really advance in this field, you need to at least be *able* to find out exactly what's going on, even if you don't always choose to do it. In addition, mistaking thoughts you have received from a guardian angel or a guide for your own on a regular basis could be detrimental to your own sense of identity – it is much better for a person to know who they really are, which is not fully possible if their own thoughts are frequently allowed to nebulously fuse with those of a discarnate.

I have identified nine ways (below, in no particular order) you can tell whether or not something comes from channelling an entity from another realm, your own intuition, or just your imagination. This is not to encourage everyone to take up channelling, because it is not something I believe everyone can or should do, but I think it will be useful for those who are wondering how to confirm their own experiences or someone else's claims.

A Nine-Point Guide to Channelling

1) *The nature of the material*
Material which is composed in a style which is completely foreign to you, which you couldn't imitate, with references you couldn't have known, or which you may not even fully agree with, is clearly coming from a source outside of yourself.

2) *Psychic experiences*
If you have a psychic experience while the material is being given, this is an indication of channelling. If you hear a sound, a voice with an accent, then you could be hearing the words of someone on another realm. An idea which pops into your head intuitively doesn't have a voice with an accent – it's coming from within you.

You may have a clairvoyant experience where you actually see the person communicating with you. This could be a definite impression in your mind, or you could actually "see" the person standing there in front of you. It may not necessarily be a person that you see, the great seer Nostradamus, for example, used to see a flame before he made the predictions he wrote in his world-renowned quatrains.

Clairsentience (psychic feeling) is when you pick up the vibe of the communicator – you sense their mood, emotions and what kind of person they are – just as you might sense people's vibes in everyday life. This is very common among mediums. Positive, dynamic, altruistic people, for example, have a strong presence and an inspiring feel about them.

Other, though much less common, psychic experiences which could happen are: psychic smell – some communicators have a certain smell about them; psychic taste – the vibe of the communicator induces the psychic sensation of taste; and a form of psychic touch, where you can actually feel something psychically almost as though it were physically there.

3) *Suspension of conscious thought*
When channelling you have to make a conscious effort to suspend your own thought. You don't exactly block out your own thoughts, but you detach your concentration from them and focus entirely on the material being received. If you start thinking about the content of the message or the phraseology used, you will lose your concentration. This does take effort, but is absolutely essential in word-for-word channelling.

4) *Intense concentration*

Intense concentration while the material is being received brings a clear awareness of whether you are indeed channelling, or whether it's your intuition, or imagination. If you concentrate on a thought, voice or image which is the product of your imagination, it will not be sustainable, whereas a genuine message or other kind of psychic experience will tend to grow in intensity the more you concentrate upon it.

Concentration when receiving a channelled message is a very intense, active state, whereas when listening to the intuition, although concentration is necessary, you are in a much more peaceful state, gently aware of a concept evolving in your mind. Concentration is like a flashlight dispelling the shadows of indiscrimination within your mind.

Channelling is, in a way, more hard work than listening to your intuition, because you have to concentrate so hard to stay in line with what you are receiving. Accessing the intuition is more of a gradual, coaxing process. It is a skill which takes a great deal of work to obtain, but once you have it, putting it into practice is, in my experience, less demanding than channelling. Of the two, there is no question that intuition is more valuable: being able to enter a deep contemplative state is a wonderful thing, which, in time, will lead to great inspiration. Intuition is an innate ability in all of us. It is a part of you. It is the voice of the essence of you. Whereas channelling is receiving something from outside of yourself, which most people don't need to do.

5) *Focusing on the words*

When most psychics receive a message they get the meaning of what is said, rather than the exact words, which most of the time is fine, but can lead to mistakes. For example, the communicator may say "drive to", and you get "go to", which are similar but distinctly different. If you are really concentrating hard, and thereby getting each word individually, you will not know what the message is about until after it's over: all your mental energy will have been focused on getting the words right, you won't have had the surplus energy to start thinking about what it means. If you do start thinking about what it means, you will lose concentration and revert to just getting the gist of the material rather than exactly what the communicator is trying to say.

Some communicators have even given me certain words letter by letter, which, though quite difficult, greatly facilitates detachment from meaning, because the letters in themselves have no meaning. So provided you manage to stay with it, just focusing on each letter as it comes, this can be an excellent way of ensuring accuracy, since any isolated mistake is usually easily detectable. It is particularly useful when an alternative word or phrase just isn't good enough – for example if I needed to get the word "pretty", and a synonym like "beautiful" wasn't acceptable, I might well be given it as P-R-E-T-T-Y.

If you manage to keep your concentration – whether it be on words or letters or a combination – you may get a whole story, or complex line of argument, which is entirely unlike anything you've ever thought. You may also get foreign words or phrases, which is very difficult indeed. In fact getting verifiable words and names which you have never heard of before is a rare skill because they are not even within your subconscious mind to draw upon. As you will see later, I have channelled poems in this way, some of which rhyme, and when it comes to rhyme, you have to get the word absolutely right – you can't make do with a similar word as you might be able to with prose.

This is completely different from writing an inspired text of your own. However inspired it is, an inspired text is still your work, and you will still have had to think it all through, whatever your state of consciousness at the time.

6) *Writing too fast to think*

If the material is coming from yourself – be it your intuition or your imagination – you have to think about it. If you are channelling something word-for-word, you often won't have time to think about it. Sometimes I find myself writing a message so fast that my hand hurts.

This is entirely different from automatic writing. In the kind of clairaudient channelling I'm talking about, although it's very fast and intense, you are the person writing. Whereas with automatic writing, the discarnate uses the medium's hand and controls it. Usually this is achieved by the medium's entering into a negative trance, thereby putting themselves totally at the mercy of the entity and unable to stop until they have finished. I do not recommend this.

7) *Synchronicity*

Sometimes the pattern and timing of events is just too extraordinary to be easily dismissed as coincidence. In terms of channelling this is when you get some kind of sign after receiving a message that the material has indeed come from another source.

In 2005, for example, I received a message from a French songwriter who had died tragically at a young age. He'd been very popular in his day and was best known for having written the tune of a classic pop song recorded by an artist who was a household name.

Directly after getting the message I went for lunch with some friends, who I had shared the experience with, to a restaurant I often go to. As I walked in, another song was being played in the restaurant by this same artist – but not the song with the tune by this songwriter. I had never heard this CD being played in the restaurant before. We listened to song after song by this artist throughout lunch – but, very disappointingly, the song in question wasn't played.

It was so tantalisingly close to being a perfect example of synchronicity that after lunch I decided to phone the restaurant and ask them what CD they had been playing and whether or not it had this song on it. I was told that the entire album in fact had the same name as the song. Synchronicity won the day.

It should be stressed that this kind of thing is helpful to the medium, and perhaps to the medium's immediate circle or to someone in some way connected to the medium's work, rather than the world at large. It gives the medium confidence that the communicator really is who they thought it was. But it doesn't prove anything on its own, and you have to be careful not to read too much into little things which might not be of any significance at all. Sometimes though the synchronicity is just too specific to ignore.

8) *Logical analysis*
This is a key point, and it simply boils down to: was the message worth getting? Has the communicator said anything worth saying?

With the best channelled material, every time you look at it you will see something you hadn't noticed before – the more you analyse the text, the more allusions and depth of meaning you will find. It should also make perfect sense, though with some more advanced material it may take you a while to fully understand it all.

9) *Intuitive assessment*

Intuition is the greatest faculty we have – our internal dial which tells us right from wrong, fact from fiction, good from bad.

If you can channel, your intuition should be good enough to tell you when you are channelling and when you're not, if not while you are receiving the material, then certainly afterwards. It should also be able to tell you something about the material.

Being a good channeller who has a poor relationship with their intuition is a bit like being a good driver who doesn't know where he is going: he can drive fast, but not necessarily in the right direction. Receiving messages from the other side is not good in itself, it's only the quality of the material that makes it good or bad, and a correct understanding of what the material is, where it's from, and how it should be used. Without a developed intuition the medium is unlikely to know the correct answers to these questions, and could even end up doing more harm than good.

In the early eighties I went through a phase of making the error of neglecting my intuition (and my logical analysis as well in fact), while still continuing to channel. Although my channelling skill didn't suffer, I ended up making some serious mistakes about the identities of the intelligences I was in touch with, thinking they were much more advanced than they were. Fortunately I had Dr King to put me straight. I felt very awkward about it at the time, but he encouraged me to continue with my psychic development, saying that we all learn from our mistakes, and that the one thing I shouldn't do was give up.

Having a good intuition is always good – whether you can channel or not. Why? Because intuition – if it really is intuition, as opposed to self-delusion or imagination – is always coming from a good place: from the spiritual part of yourself.

This is by far the most important of these nine points.

* * *

Channelling is a global phenomenon. It is extremely interesting to note that similar experiences relating to psychic contact with discarnates are known in cultures all over the world – sometimes even virtually identical specific details can be found in traditions which have grown up entirely independently of one another at opposite ends of the globe, indicating that certain fundamental principles of inter-realm communication do indeed exist.

CHAPTER 3

Ancestors

"...those immortal dead who live again
In minds made better by their presence"
George Eliot

In 1978 I went to New Zealand to do a tour promoting various spiritual concepts. The strength of Maori influence in terms of psychic activity hit me as soon as I got off the plane.

I was staying in Auckland, but had a TV interview lined up in Wellington – a plane ride away. On arrival at Wellington's small airport I found my driver holding a sign with my name on it. He was a young, tall, stocky, smartly dressed Maori, with a driver's peaked cap. I said hello and he told me his name.

At this point an elderly Maori gentleman came up to him, evidently having overheard his name, and proceeded to tell him, at length, the history of his family going back several generations. This aroused a great deal of interest and respect from my driver, and he asked him to join us in the car.

The gentleman's name was Captain Tenga Rangi, known to his friends as Bill. He turned out to be the chief "Tohunga" (a Maori with various traditional skills and areas of knowledge) of the Rotorua district of New Zealand. The previous week he had met a senior German politician as a representative of his people in some official engagement. The German politician had addressed him in Maori, and he had replied in German – an exchange which had deeply impressed everyone.

"It's funny, actually I was hoping to meet a Tohunga…" I began, casually.

"I know," he interrupted.

We continued chatting, and he actually volunteered to come into the TV studio with me while I did the interview – an offer which I accepted. He was very supportive and gave me lots of useful advice.

When I went back to New Zealand in 1982, I returned to Rotorua and met up with him. He was in the process of training his nephew to be his successor, which necessitated the two of them being together virtually all the time. They were driving around the district in his large Cadillac-like car, and invited me to join them and show me round. During this trip he felt inspired to tell me the secrets of one of their rituals, despite the fact that I was not Maori.

I was the first non-Maori he'd ever initiated in this way. He made me swear never to reveal the details of the initiation – a secrecy I have maintained. However, I will say that the principles of their form of ancestor communication bore a remarkable resemblance to Western Spiritualism.

* * *

Belief in life after death breaks virtually every barrier of time and space.

It is part of the human psyche – and has been for millennia. Personally, I have no doubt that it goes back to the very dawn of human civilisation, but even in academic circles it is believed to perhaps go back as far as 50,000 BC. Since there are no written records from that period, this belief is evidenced by the way corpses were disposed of. Palaeolithic peoples, including the Neanderthals, not only went to the trouble of burying the bodies of those who had passed on, but also gave them such things as food, ornaments and weapons – implying a belief that such things remained useful in a spiritual sense, even after they could no longer be used in a physical way. In addition, skeletons have been known to be found crouching on their sides, like a foetus in the womb, which could be interpreted as indicating a belief in rebirth of some kind.

And today virtually every society on Earth believes in life after death in some form, many believing that communication with the "dead" (who are of course very much alive) is possible, and in some cases even necessary to the survival of the living.

This is particularly associated with *Shamanism*. The word "shaman" comes from a northeast Asian word, deriving from the verb "*ša-*", "to know". Literally it means "he who knows" – a fitting description for someone who would indeed know considerably more about life after death than the other members of his (or her) social group, and in fact vastly more than most of our educated minds in modern Western "civilisation".

It is hard to pin down exactly what Shamanism is, in that it is to be found in different forms all over the world. In this chapter I am treating it in its loosest possible sense to refer to the ideology or techniques of any technologically undeveloped culture which tie in with communication with discarnates. In the strictest sense of the word, such figures as medicine men are not regarded as shamans because their knowledge can be learnt through deliberate study.

A true shaman, typified in various Siberian ethnic groups, has no choice in their calling. They are called not by their own inner voice, but by the "spirits". The fact that they are born to their role is indicated by certain physical characteristics, such as an extra tooth or finger, or some kind of unusual mark. In some cases it is thought they may have "inherited" the soul of a deceased shaman. Their destiny apparently unavoidable, they may go through a period of illness, during which time it is thought that the spirits are forcing the young shaman-to-be into a willingness to cooperate. Only upon surrender will the illness cease. There is a case of a Nivkh shaman (southeastern Siberia) who is reported to have said he would have died if he hadn't become a shaman.

A shaman may be taught by the spirits themselves; they need to acquire an extensive array of psychic powers such as the ability to locate a lost animal or to combat infertility. A shaman is also often expected to be able to enter into what is loosely termed "ecstasy", which I would regard as probably being some kind of a trance condition. In this state, either a spirit speaks through the shaman, or the shaman vacates his body and visits one of the "spirit realms".

In Eskimo culture the ability to leave one's body is key to the function of the shaman, or *angakok*. Some shamans claim to have flown around the Earth and even been to the moon. Such abilities of course give a shaman considerable power and prestige within the community, the more ambitious claims doubtless given credibility by success in more earthly pursuits, such as healing the sick. In fact the Eskimo word *angajkok*, meaning "leader" is related to the word for shaman. Likewise the shamans of South America have great authority, gained through their renowned healing abilities, as well as other powers, such as being able to guide someone who has just died to their new realm. However, the shaman's status is not entirely unquestioned, as is reflected by the somewhat sardonic saying among the Altai Kizhi, an ethnic group indigenous to the Altai Mountains in Central Asia – if a beast gets sick, the dogs get fat; if a man gets sick, the shaman gets fat.

Healing is an important part of Shamanism. The various ways of curing illness are as diverse as their potential cause. However, as we might expect in cultures to which modern medicine was alien, both the cause and cure of illness were often considered to be what we might term "supernatural". For example in many cultures illness might be the result of violating a taboo or be caused by a mischievous spirit. Likewise spirits are involved in the healing of disease, such as among the Ladakhi people of the Himalayas.

According to *National Geographic* (online) the *lhapa* and *lhamo* – male and female "oracles" – claim to heal patients while a spirit takes them over, or "possesses" them, which generally only happens after several minutes of a combination of chanting, praying, drumming, bell-ringing, incense-burning and swaying backwards and forwards, though possession can sometimes take place without the *lhapa* or *lhamo's* consent. The spirit is frequently identified as a Buddhist deity – but could also be thought to be an intelligence associated with another faith, or the spirit's identity could be left open. The majority of the oracles themselves are Buddhists, though they have patients of various different religious backgrounds, including Hindus and Christians.

The whole process can make a wild spectacle. The oracle may shout at or even strike the patient in an attempt to exorcise an evil spirit, or suck the condition from the patient's body through pipes or straws, afterwards spitting out what sometimes looks like black mucus. They may also hit, or even use swords to cut, their own bodies.

In contrast, a little further East, in Confucianism, which is native to China but influential elsewhere in Asia, although there is a kind of ancestor worship, it is based on the idea that ritual creates order in society rather than on Shamanistic principles. The great sage Confucius (551-479 BC) himself is recorded as having been unwilling to talk about what happened after death, or indeed about anything remotely "paranormal". However, in practice, in China what remnants of ancestor worship still exist have become intermingled with Buddhist mythology. For example, you can still buy "money" which is burnt supposedly in order to release it into the realm of the deceased where it can be used to buy things. The reasons for this kind of behaviour in modern China seem, however, to have more to do with expressing grief for the departed than with seriously-held views on life after death.

Although African religion – in all its many different forms – is not normally associated with Shamanism, concepts of healing and contact with discarnates are indeed key to many native beliefs. The revering of ancestors is common – in both a positive and a negative sense. The word "ancestor" may not be used in the way that we use it, to mean any relative who has died. It would seem that to be an "ancestor" in traditional African ideology you have to have led a worthy life. As well as providing access to spiritual guidance and power, these ancestors are also enforcers of morality. If someone suffers misfortune or illness, it could well be regarded as the result of some kind of moral failing, for which they are being punished by their ancestors.

However, when I went to Nigeria in 1980, what struck me was not the differences between native beliefs and my own, but the similarities.

I was a guest of the Deputy Governor of Rivers State, who was a keen supporter of Aetherius Society work. As a prominent figure in

Nigeria, he was able to introduce me to a host of chiefs, governors, deputy governors and other important people, and I was driven from place to place in a grand procession of cars and outriders – a novel experience indeed!

I was asked if there was anything I particularly wanted to do while I was there which wasn't already on our schedule. There was – to see a typical Nigerian village.

We drove along an earth road to the village where my host had grown up. It was everything you might expect: mud huts, brightly dressed women carrying huge jars on their heads, people sitting in doorways pounding yam – the staple food there, and bright-eyed children staring with friendly curiosity at what was probably the first white person they had ever seen.

I was asked to give a lecture, which of course I was only too happy to do. This was to take place in a meeting area they called their "town hall", which was a large square building with benches on each of its four sides and a centre stage. The most unusual thing about it was that it didn't have a roof – though this hardly mattered in the African sunshine, which thankfully wasn't too hot that day.

Despite the fact that hardly anyone in the village could speak English, every single one of them – men and women, old and young, totalling around two hundred people – came along to hear me speak.

I spoke for about twenty minutes, during which they listened with unwavering attention, followed by rapturous applause. When I had finished, the local seer, or "native doctor" as they called him, stood up and talked for a few minutes in the local language, which of course I didn't understand. This was again followed by thunderous applause.

Afterwards I was told that he had been explaining that while I was speaking he had had a wonderful psychic vision of golden light, and wished to thank me because they had "indeed been blessed by God this day to have heard such a wonderful message" – or something to that effect. A very touching tribute, I felt, especially since he hadn't understood a single word.

Such a vision is unlikely to have anything to do with me. It would almost certainly have been to do with the spiritual content of my lecture, which would have attracted the interest of various higher forces who wished to help the villagers understand what I was saying.

* * *

Just as in any field of endeavour, I'm sure there are fakes who are consciously lying about their experiences – more showman than shaman – and indeed people who are deluding themselves. However, the full picture is likely to be much more complicated. For example, many of the experiences reported may be genuine, but exaggerated. It may be that the shaman does not always fully understand what he has experienced, but, under pressure from those around him, is forced to come up with an explanation. Or perhaps a single experience may be a combination of genuine psychic perception and hallucination.

I have great respect for many aspects of Shamanism, particularly working with healing "spirits", or "guides", but I would regard the practices used by some shamans as unsafe. The use of drugs and negative trance in particular, and all practices in which the shaman loses control, while they may be effective in certain ways, can be extremely dangerous.

Nevertheless – dangerous or not – shamanic practice, and the belief systems and techniques associated with it, do demonstrate the universality of the phenomenon of communication with the other realms. However this should not lead you to the conclusion that all mediums are alike, or differ only in the their preferred means of communication. On the contrary, just as with any skill, there is a huge range of *ability*.

CHAPTER 4

Mediums

"The dead don't die. They look on and help"
D. H. Lawrence

No medium, or psychic of any kind, is 100% accurate, whatever method they use, and anyone who tells you that they are is in serious trouble. It is essential in psychic development, and indeed in development of any kind, to know your weaknesses, stay grounded, have a good sense of humour, be questioning, be humble, and not take yourself too seriously.

Some people think that you are either psychic or you're not, and that if you are then you know everything from the meaning of life to where your next-door neighbour has left her car keys. This is ridiculous. No psychic knows everything. Being psychic – whatever form it may take, be it intuitive, mediumistic, clairsentient, etc. – is just a way of accessing certain information – how much, and how accurately you can access it depends on how good a psychic you are.

Messages from the other side are always, to some extent, prone to being affected by the medium's own thoughts, no matter how hard they might be trying to prevent this.

Other than general mental clutter and lack of concentration, the medium's emotions can play a big role in distorting a message. One manifestation of this is, what I call, the "Father Christmas Complex". This is a compulsive desire to bestow "gifts", motivated, usually unconsciously, either by a sense of generosity, or by the desire to be a more popular, and therefore potentially wealthier, medium: "I see a lot of money coming your way… and that Ferrari's not far off… your children will be exceptionally intelligent… love's just around the corner…" This can be exacerbated by the psychic telepathically tuning in to the thoughts of the sitter (person receiving the reading), mistaking what the sitter *wants* to happen for what *will* happen. Every psychic and medium needs to learn to detach from the hopes, dreams and fears of their sitter, and recognise the origin of each psychic impression they pick up – a feat which is easier said than done.

On a more basic level, personal values will often affect a medium or psychic. For example, a morally upright medium, perhaps from a conservative Christian background, who gets a message that their sitter is having an affair with a married man is likely to have a very different stance to a more liberally minded medium who believes that everyone should "follow their feelings providing nobody gets hurt".

But accuracy alone is not the measure of a good medium – you should also take into account the quality of the message received. I have met some brilliant mediums who receive astoundingly accurate messages, but very often these messages are utterly banal, relating to trivial matters such as interior décor or plumbing. Such people would not be capable of receiving a message from a more advanced intelligence giving spiritual teaching. On the other hand you could have a spiritually advanced individual on a much higher level of perception who was not nearly as accurate a medium. If you are both very accurate and able to obtain a high spiritual level, you are truly a great medium.

Think of a medium as being like a sieve. Most mediums would be like sieves with very small holes, coarse mesh and probably a bit of grime as well. Only small, trivial bits of information can get through, and when they do, they are often discoloured by the grime. Occasionally, however, you find a medium who is like a sieve with large holes and very fine mesh. Such people can receive substantial, high quality information, which the first type of medium could not. They could also get the trivial stuff as well, but they wouldn't choose to, because this would lower their vibrations and, over time, could even cause them to lose the ability to receive material of a higher calibre.

The general principle is that mediums can only receive information from entities who live in a state of consciousness similar to that which the medium is capable of achieving, although the medium would not live in this state of consciousness all the time. Personally, I find it requires a huge effort on my part to raise my consciousness sufficiently to communicate with more advanced guides. However it is essential during the communication process to reach the level of consciousness they require.

Normally a very advanced intelligence would not have any wish to communicate through a basic medium because that medium wouldn't know how to deal with the information given. And if such an intelligence tried to communicate directly with such a medium, it could actually be dangerous for the medium.

However I do believe that it is possible for a more advanced intelligence on a higher realm to convey a message to a medium through one or more intermediaries on the realm or realms between the advanced intelligence's realm and our own creating a kind of human chain of communication, but the original message would inevitably be prone to modification and distortion in the process.

Dr King's mediumship was like a clean sieve with hardly any

mesh at all – meaning that he could receive extremely advanced information with virtually no discolouration whatsoever. This kind of ability is rare to the point of being unique – an example channellers should all strive towards.

* * *

How all this affects you depends on your goals – on whether you are a medium/psychic, someone who would like to be a medium/psychic, or someone who is just reading for general interest.

The first piece of advice I would give to everyone is: develop your intuition. Don't say you haven't got time. Make time. A good intuition will save you hours, perhaps years, or even lives. Think about it: if you have a good intuition you will make better decisions, you will go through life with eyes open, saving you from bumping into unpleasant disappointments – it can help you make the right decision with regard to every aspect of your life, from what car you should buy, to who you should marry, to what spiritual path to follow – decisions which if made wrongly can lead to a huge amount of unnecessary suffering.

Motive is very important in any spiritual or psychic development. If your only motive is your own personal success and happiness, chances are you won't get very far. In channelling, the purity of one's motive can usually be equated to the cleanliness or mesh structure of the sieve. With intuition, quality of motive is even more crucial. Intuition is a pure, untarnished force within you – your hotline to the Divine – and it responds best to a pure, untarnished motive. If you want to use your intuition to help others, and you cultivate the patience necessary to do this, you can make rapid strides forwards.

Before anyone even thinks about trying to channel, they should have a good motive, sound mental health, sound emotional health, no problem with drug or alcohol abuse, a good intuition, and good concentration, and be actively involved in some kind of service to others. Without these seven strengths, it is all too possible to get deluded – either believing they are channelling when they are not, or making serious mistakes about the identity of the communicator, or content of the material. In some cases, a student could attract the wrong kind of entity, which could even lead to possession, which I will talk more about in Chapter 6.

In the majority of cases, it's not worth the risk.

In addition, I cannot stress strongly enough the importance of controlling the imagination. There are those who believe they are hearing "voices" who are in fact schizophrenic, and those who are classified schizophrenic who are in fact having uncontrolled psychic experiences. That is why I recommend the discipline of a spiritual development programme based on yoga principles with concentration at its heart. Those suffering from a delusional form of mental illness shouldn't even consider channelling unless they have completely cured this problem within themselves.

Developing your intuition, on the other hand, is much, much safer, and the best way I know of doing it is to practise the techniques in the book *Realise Your Inner Potential*, which I was privileged to co-author with Dr King. These spiritual practices really are second to none. I'm not just saying that because I co-wrote the book. I don't receive any royalties from it – all royalties go to The Aetherius Society, which is a non-profit organisation. I'm saying it because I and countless others have practised these techniques, all of which were taught by Dr King, for many years and I know they work. Based mainly on ancient yoga philosophy, they are not all unique, some are old and some are new, but whatever their origin, they work in a gentle, balanced, natural way without requiring force of any kind – and pose no risk to anyone who practises them as taught.

Likewise, if you are already a practising psychic or medium, you will find these techniques invaluable in enhancing concentration, discrimination, protection, detachment etc. They will also take you from just being psychic, to being genuinely spiritual. Some people mix the two up, but they can be very, very different. You can be extremely spiritual with virtually no psychic ability at all, and very unspiritual with excellent psychic ability. Of the two, it is far better to be spiritual: spirituality is an awareness of the Divinity within and a conscious effort to live and act in the light of this knowledge by devoting your life in service to others.

It is not necessary or even advisable for everyone to develop psychic abilities in the way that I chose to. In fact, psychic development can be a distraction from the all-important spiritual path of service to others and, in the final analysis, the only valid use of your psychic abilities is to help others. One way or another all spiritual students will have psychic experiences, but to what extent and in what way depends entirely on their own individual development, and indeed on the type of service they are called to give.

If you decide to go to a psychic for a reading, provided you don't take it all too seriously and treat every word they say as divine prophecy, it can be helpful. They should be able to give you good evidence that they are genuine, but you are wasting their time if you refuse to tell them anything at all, and expect them to know everything. It's like going to the doctor. When the doctor asks you what's wrong, you don't say, "Well, you're the doctor – you tell me." That would be absurd, achieving nothing but limiting how much the doctor was able to help you. It's just the same when having a reading done.

You should, however, bear in mind that just because someone is mediumistic, it doesn't mean they are wise. Even if they are accurate in what they get, they may still give you poor advice – a good psychic will make it clear what they're getting psychically, and what is their own opinion. However, even then – even if the medium is extremely accurate – unless they really know what they are doing, they may bring through a discarnate who, though well-intentioned, may well not be particularly wise either. It could be your Auntie Gladys, who you never took any notice of while she was alive. She's probably learnt a thing or two since her passing, not least that there is life after death, but, be aware that she is still Auntie Gladys!

Many people have their own guardian angels or spirit guides, watching over them from the other side, who may or may not be people they have known while they were alive. As well as giving guidance, which you might not be consciously aware of without contacting a medium, they can also offer protection. I was told of a case of a man driving his car whose hands, holding the steering wheel, were mysteriously given a gentle nudge. Had they not been, it is his belief that he would have had a fatal accident.

When I used to give a lot of psychic readings I was surprised at just how many guides were Native Americans – considering that there aren't that many Native Americans in the world, nor have there ever been. I can only presume that it is because their culture traditionally embraces the concept of spirit guides. I have also come across a high percentage of spirit guides who were nuns, particularly Sisters of Mercy. Although they no longer hold on to some of the dogmatic beliefs they would have held while incarnate as nuns on this realm, they still wear a habit, possibly to make a connection with this realm. The habit is usually white, though sometimes pale blue or light grey; I have never seen one in black. Sometimes they wear a cross, though never a crucifix, and more than once I have seen a very wide white bonnet. They often have a particular interest in healing.

Sometimes, rather than being a source of guidance, a medium is used to contact a loved one who has recently passed on in order to bring about closure. This can be a very healing experience for both you and the deceased – a final chance to say whatever was left unsaid, or, indeed, an attempt to unsay whatever had been said...

CHAPTER 5

Closure

"In my end is my beginning"
Mary, Queen of Scots

"I wish you were dead!" she screamed.

Why, I don't know. Sometimes it's best not to ask. All I know is: Mrs Jones was very, very angry when she said these words to her husband.

A week later she called me in a terrible state. Her husband had died. Could I help?

* * *

Contacting deceased loved ones is not always a good idea, and isn't something that generally I like to do. After death, following an initial period of adjustment on the part of the person who has died, and of grieving on the part of those left behind, both parties should move on to other things – especially the deceased. Although this realm offers us the biggest challenges in terms of the rough and tumble of experience, the basic spirit realms and above offer us the opportunity to learn more about life's subtleties and, of course, prepare for our next life. Spiritual teaching is much more readily available and easily assimilatable, and there are fewer distractions to deflect us from what is really important. There is also the opportunity to do fantastic spiritual work, such as guiding bewildered secular materialists and confused orthodox minds through the transition process.

Any discarnate who ignores this, and simply does their best to stay in touch with the physical realm and all its worries is seriously missing out on a wonderful opportunity to evolve. If you are one of those people who has a reading every month with a medium who can put you in touch with Uncle Pete, a bit like having a monthly long-distance phone call to a relative who has emigrated to Australia, you aren't doing Uncle Pete any favours – nor is he doing you any. Both of you should be focusing on the affairs of the realms you are on. Everything happens for a reason: if you were meant to be in regular contact with Uncle Pete, you wouldn't be living on different realms.

I once went to a Spiritualist church where a member of the congregation was told by a medium that her Aunt Mabel thought she should get her plumbing fixed or some such triviality. This is an abuse of mediumship. Communication between the realms should not be used to convey advice or information of such a basic nature: it merely serves to perpetuate the discarnate's attachment to the physical realm and thereby hinder their spiritual advancement. In addition, there is unfortunately often a tendency for the relative on this realm to think that such a message or instruction carries great authority, consequently treating it with vastly more importance than it deserves, in the most extreme of cases even to the point of neglecting responsibilities on this realm in order to carry out the wishes of someone on a another realm.

Some people become hopelessly dependent on their discarnate relatives – or on discarnates in general. This was illustrated to me very clearly on one occasion before I had even become psychic, when I was invited by the medium mentioned in Chapter 2 – the lady who had said she had seen Sir Oliver Lodge – over to her house for dinner.

We had a very pleasant evening. She even entertained her husband and me by playing improvised channelled music on her grand piano. It got late, and it was a dark, wet winter's evening, so she asked me to stay the night, which I did. Just as I was about to go up to bed she gave me a bucket. Seeing my puzzled expression, she explained what it was for – "You'll need this for the leak in the roof." And indeed I did.

The following morning over breakfast, she announced in total seriousness that she had received word "from spirit" that she should get the hole in the roof repaired. Her husband nodded appreciatively and agreed that if that's what spirit wanted that's what they should do.

Even at the time as a young guy with no apparent mediumistic abilities, I remember thinking that the whole situation was absurd. Anyone with an ounce of common sense could have told them to get the roof mended – but they needed to hear it "from spirit". It is common sense that no one should become so hopelessly dependent on guidance from above that they lose the ability to make decisions by themselves.

This may come as a shock to many readers, and is likely to prove unpopular with some, but it is too important to ignore. Dr King was certainly of this opinion, and so are my own guides. One venerable and scholarly gentleman, who I believe was a psychic researcher in his last life, gave me quite a long message about his uncompromising feelings on this whole subject.

However, brief communication with a deceased loved one shortly after death can be helpful in sorting out unresolved issues, healing emotional wounds, and, of course, proves to the person left behind that the deceased is still alive, which is both comforting and serves as an important spiritual lesson, especially to someone who doesn't believe in life after death.

To my mind Mrs Jones' plight was a classic case where it would indeed be perfectly acceptable to try to contact the deceased.

We sat down in the rather aging armchairs of one of our upstairs offices and began to talk about what had happened. He had died out of the blue of a heart attack or something similar, which meant his death had come as a terrible shock – a shock compounded by the terrible guilt she felt about her harsh words. A lesson to never say anything in the heat of passion – but a lesson too late for Mrs Jones (not her real name of course).

As we talked, I began to be aware of, and then to see, a plump middle-aged man with an alarmingly red face kneeling in front of his wife pleading for forgiveness – a sight which surprised me since I had been led to believe that it was she who wanted to beg *him* for forgiveness. Presumably he was begging for forgiveness for whatever he had done which had caused his wife to say that she wished him dead. They duly forgave one another and the guilt of both parties was put to an end.

When dealing with the bereaved, as well as accuracy and quality, another important skill that every medium should have is of course empathy. You have to make the effort to understand the sitter's problems or grief in order to convey whatever it is you are getting in a sympathetic way – rather than just blurting out whatever comes to you like a robot. In fact I believe that every psychic who does regular readings of any kind could benefit immensely from some sort of counselling training. Likewise, counsellors could benefit immensely from training in basic psychic development, so they could learn to tune in to their patients on an intuitive level rather than just having to rely on what they are told. Some counsellors, I believe, driven purely by the concentrated desire to help their patients, do in fact develop an intuitive degree of empathy, without even realising it.

In an ideal world of course we would all be able to counsel ourselves out of whatever problems we had, and similarly we would be able to make any occasional contact with the other side which we genuinely needed to make without requiring a medium to do it for us. And indeed it does sometimes happen that people who wouldn't consider themselves to be psychic are somehow able to communicate with the deceased in a safe, natural way – albeit only briefly – in their sleep.

A few years ago a Nigerian friend of mine lost his mother, causing all the normal grief that one would expect to accompany such a loss. Just after her passing he had had a dream, in which his mother had spoken to him explaining various aspects of her will, including names of places he had never heard of – right down to quite specific details of an address. He woke up and could remember everything very clearly. It seemed a strange dream to have had; he hadn't even been thinking about his mother's will – and what she had told him seemed a bit far-fetched.

It was only when her will was read out a while later that everything fell into place. It even referred to the places he had been told about in the dream. In fact, he was very grateful for having had the dream – without it he would have been left extremely confused.

This, I believe, was an out of body experience: my friend left his body and met his mother. Though an experience of this level of clarity is unusual, going to sleep with a problem in your mind and waking up with an answer is very common. Of course this is often simply a result of the subconscious cogitating in peace, released from the distractions of the waking state, but in some cases it could be that a guardian angel aware of your situation has given you a helping hand.

Similar to the "out of body" phenomenon is the classic "near death experience". This is when someone technically dies and briefly leaves their body. Some even hear someone pronouncing them dead. Details vary, but generally the person moves along a dark tunnel towards a bright light, often to be met by apparently angelic beings. The reason for returning to the body is often the realisation that there is work still to be done in this life on this realm. Following recovery from whatever illness or accident prompted the experience, many people adopt a more spiritual outlook and make positive changes in their lives. The number of people coming close to death who report this phenomenon totals literally millions.

Sometimes people see guardian angels just before they die, without leaving the body, as though their consciousness is gradually attuning itself to the realm for which it is destined. The great artist Thomas Gainsborough's (1727-1788) last words are recorded to have been: "We are all going to Heaven, and Van Dyck is of the company", suggesting a clairvoyant experience in which he saw Van Dyck (1599-1641) coming to meet him.

* * *

Belief in guardian angels, in whatever form, or contact with deceased loved ones is nothing new. In Winchester Cathedral there is a Guardian Angels' Chapel, the vault (ceiling) of which was painted with depictions of angels in 1241 by a man named Master William on the instructions of King Henry III. More recently, Queen Victoria is recorded as having had an interest in Spiritualism – though it is not known to what extent this was prompted by the death of her beloved husband, Prince Albert, who died of typhoid fever in 1861.

The radical new ideology known as "Spiritualism" had been sparked off by the press interest surrounding the mysterious goings-on in the Fox family cottage in the small hamlet of Hydesville, New York, just 13 years before Albert's death. Contact with the spirit world had, of course, been going on for millennia, but this is how it was largely brought to the fore in the modern Western world.

Mr John Fox, a blacksmith by trade, was a former alcoholic who had managed to change his ways and become teetotal. He was a quiet man, and his wife, Margaret, good-natured. They had their youngest two children quite late in life. They were simple, ordinary Methodists who would never in a million years have guessed what a stir these two little girls – the charming Margaretta and pretty Catherine, known as Maggie and Kate or Cathie – were destined to cause, not just in the neighbourhood, but throughout the world.

They had been hearing strange noises like the sound of someone knocking ever since they had moved into their dilapidated wooden homestead just before Christmas 1847. The source of the sounds remained elusive, despite Mr and Mrs Fox's best investigative efforts.

One Friday night the following March the whole family, utterly drained by the strange goings-on, went to bed just after 6pm, to be woken again by the sound of knocking. Seven-year-old Kate, addressing the knocker as "Mr Splitfoot", possibly an allusion to the hooves of the traditional orthodox Christian image of the devil, brazenly invited him to copy her as she clapped her hands. As soon as she had finished, they heard the same number of knocks, or "raps" as they are often called. Then ten-year-old Maggie clapped "one, two, three, four", again inviting the knocker to copy her, which he did. Mrs Fox, then asked him to "rap" her children's ages, which again he did. The sentiency of the knocker clearly established, Mrs Fox asked if he was a spirit – two raps for yes. Two raps followed.

Several neighbours were asked to come round and see, or rather "hear", for themselves the unusual activity. They continued asking the "spirit" questions, receiving answers that met with their satisfaction.

It turned out that the discarnate was a peddler called Charles B. Rosna who had been robbed and murdered in the house with a butcher's knife earlier in the decade.

As can be imagined, all this excitement took its toll on the Fox family. Mrs Fox's hair reportedly turned white within a few days. Margaretta was sent to stay with her sister, Leah Fish, a single-mother who had survived by making a living teaching music, while Kate was dispatched to the home of another sibling. However, perhaps because the girls had come up with the idea of communicating with the discarnate, the phenomenon followed them, as well as continuing in the family cottage. In fact things got worse, as the raps turned into typical poltergeist activity, with incidents ranging from annoying to dangerous, such as blocks of wood flying around. Strange as it may sound, however, it was a while before they thought to try to converse with the cause of these happenings, as they had managed to do successfully back in Hydesville.

As soon as they did, answers began to come, including a message urging them to tell the world about spirit communication. They were investigated and no signs of fraud were detected. However, many of the mediums who were appearing as a result of the publicity surrounding the Fox family, were indeed exposed as charlatans. In this hostile climate the Fox sisters themselves also suffered accusations of fakery. Later, the sisters, plagued by financial problems, alcoholism and quarrelling, reached rock bottom when Margaretta "confessed" to being a fraud – a confession she later retracted, apparently with bitter remorse.

Leah, who some believe had taken what had originally been Maggie and Kate's childish prank and ruthlessly exploited it at her sisters' expense, did very well out of Spiritualism, ending up a sought-after medium with a wealthy husband. Alcoholics Maggie and Kate, however, died in dire poverty. Controversy still surrounds the tragic story today – many believing the whole thing to have been a money-making scheme, inspired by varying degrees of greed or indigence. Whatever the truth of it – the sisters' impact on attitudes to modern mediumship is not in doubt.

Amidst all this excitement in such a staid period of Western cultural history, it is not surprising that Queen Victoria is said to have sought to use Spiritualism to reunite her with her husband, whom she grieved to the point of obsession.

It has been reported that, shortly after Albert died, a 13-year-old boy called Robert James Lees, was contacted by a discarnate purporting to be the Prince, during a séance which had taken place with his family and a local newspaper editor. The editor published this information and it came to Queen Victoria's attention, following which she dispatched two people (using false names) to investigate.

Lees was again contacted by the Prince, who recognised both the investigators and revealed their real names. He also used the boy to write a letter to the Queen, in which he called his wife a pet name which no one else had known.

Intrigued, she asked Lees to conduct a séance at Windsor Castle. So impressed was she at his abilities that he was invited back several times and even offered permanent employment, which he declined as a result of the advice given to him by his spirit guide.

* * *

As far as methods of contact with ordinary discarnates is concerned, I have covered the good and the bad. Regrettably I must now look at the *ugly*.

CHAPTER 6

Exorcisms

"Rise up, and bathe the world in light!"
William Wordsworth

I didn't play a very big part in my first exorcism, it was led by a more experienced colleague and I was just one of two junior assistants.

There was psychic interference going on in a shop just down the road. It was run by a married couple who lived upstairs with their adolescent daughter. Mysterious phenomena such as doors locking by themselves, strange noises, including voices, and foul stenches had caused tremendous distress and disruption to their lives, turning the wife into a virtual nervous wreck. Everything had been fine till one Christmas they had thought it would be "fun" to play with a ouija board. A name was spelt out. The next day the husband went to the library and looked up the name, discovering that a person by that name had indeed lived in the area hundreds of years ago and committed suicide. "How amazing!" he had thought to himself.

Foolish. Foolish. Foolish. Sold as a party game to pass the time after dinner on a boring winter's evening, the ouija board is DANGEROUS. I would advise you to stay well clear of it because I've seen what can happen. It can act as a gateway for discarnates, which can be perfectly OK, but can be disastrous. It's a bit like leaving your front door wide open – you might be fine, an old friend might even pop in to see you, but then again so might a mad axe murderer. In fact in some ways it is more dangerous than leaving your front door open, because mischievous discarnates sometimes have certain powers which people on this realm do not – such as the ability to lock doors while remaining totally invisible to the ordinary eye.

The three of us went down there and did the usual sort of thing – blessing the walls, chanting mantras, saying prayers in a powerful way, doing certain visualisations etc.

At that time I wasn't psychic and I didn't see anything. But I do know that the smells, the noises and the spontaneous door-locking stopped immediately afterwards.

The first time I actually had the experience of seeing an "interfering entity", for want of a better term, was a few years later in a hotel room. I was away on important spiritual business for Dr King, and the more spiritual the work you do, the more likely it is that some kind of interference will take place, whether you are aware of it or not. I have no evidence that this was actually what was happening on this occasion – it could have just been a malicious entity which had some connection with the building I was staying in and happened to stumble across me – or it could have been a bit of both.

I didn't see its features, I could just see a dark presence and "feel" it.

A few seconds later I became aware of the towering figure of a Native American spirit guide, who slowly, but very surely, boomed out: "Leave – this – boy – ALO-O-O-NE!"

The dark presence scarpered in terror, only to be followed by the powerful guide who wasted no time in running after it. This was clearly a man who didn't half-do anything: he wanted to be absolutely sure that I was left in peace. A part of me feels I shouldn't say this, since it seems a bit flippant, but the whole scene reminded me of a cartoon, and struck me as almost comical, despite its serious nature. That's the best way I can describe it – the speed, the directness, the unquestioning responses – it wasn't like anything we encounter in our daily lives on this realm.

Who the dark presence was exactly, I never knew, but I did find a good deal out about interference, a field in which Dr King had unmatchable expertise. I have also subsequently learnt a lot about entities who have died, but still reside in this realm, often described as ghosts.

The first point to make is that there is no such thing as a demon, though in fact my wife, Alyson, did actually clairvoyantly see what looked like a demon in our room one night while we were on holiday in Wales – unlikely though that may sound! She described it as being like a strange, monstrous animal, with eagle-like talons – a dark, solid mass, with a barely perceptible reddish glow around it; most sinister of all being its large, hollow, soulless eyes – like pits of blackness.

I couldn't see it, I'm glad to say, but I could feel its creepy presence. She tried mantra and visualisation techniques but nothing seemed to work, so in the end she told it to clear off in no uncertain terms, which, amazingly, it did – sort of disintegrating and dematerialising all at once. Perhaps it was daunted by her lack of fear. Straight after that the fire alarm went off for no apparent reason and we all had to assemble outside. It wasn't a drill and there wasn't a fire – but things like that can and do sometimes happen in a climate of psychic interference. On returning to our room we did some spiritual practices and didn't have any more trouble.

We had been warned by Dr King the previous day to be on guard for interference on this trip, and as always he was spot on.

Unbeknown to me, he was at that time seeking permission from a higher spiritual authority to give his wife, Monique, and myself a very special Initiation, about which there is a little more in Chapters 7 and 10. I have little doubt that the interference was spurred by this move.

It had probably adopted the guise of a demon specifically in order to scare Alyson, or people in general. Some malefic entities thrive on the negative energy of fear and actually use it to boost their own power. Seeing that it had failed in its main objective probably made it lose confidence and give up.

There is no possibility that it could have been a real "demon" – in the orthodox sense of the term. There is no such thing as an entity which is totally evil – though some come close. Every being in creation – from a God to a sadistic dictator – has a Divine Spark within them. No matter how low anyone may fall, their situation is never hopeless. Even the worst of the worst will eventually rise up from whatever depths of unconscionable depravity they may have sunk to, and evolve towards God-consciousness – the goal of all life.

However, this does not make malevolent entities any the less dangerous. Trying to make a malevolent entity see reason through patient diplomacy is as unlikely to have any effect as sweet-talking a psychopath.

Troublesome discarnates are people who have lived here just like you or I, but, upon dying, have either failed to pass on properly for some reason, or have passed on successfully and reside on another realm but still seek to cause trouble on this one. Entities in the first category are usually called "ghosts" though this term is often used more loosely these days.

Ghost sightings are not uncommon. According to *The Telegraph* (online), actress Joanna Lumley was told by a ghost attired in workman's clothes to vacate her own home – and she did indeed end up selling her house and moving. Many tales of ghosts relate to famous old buildings – Henry VIII's palace, Hampton Court, apparently being a bit of a hotspot for spooky goings on, including stories relating to two of his six wives, Catherine Howard, who he had executed, and Jane Seymour, who died in childbirth. A few years ago, it was even claimed that a ghost had been caught on CCTV.

It is the second category of entity which is generally the more sinister of the two. Such an entity would be living on one of "the lower astral realms" – the four realms below the physical realm – sometimes referred to as "the hells", though this term would paint a very inaccurate picture in most people's minds. They are not filled with lakes of boiling sulphur, but they are very unpleasant, filled with the worst dregs of humanity. In places they might be a bit like some of the less pleasant parts of this realm, filled with sad souls who have wasted their lives – either in deliberately immoral activity like robbery or mugging, or by squandering their opportunities to advance because they were drug addicts or alcoholics, or just by failing to make use of their opportunities to help others – one of the worst crimes of all, depending on your potential.

The case of the interference in the local shop in the Fulham Road is likely to fall into the first category – someone who has failed to pass on properly – which would mean that the ouija board had somehow served to trigger into action a presence which was already there. He was a man who had committed suicide, so he clearly wasn't in a good emotional state when he died. This could well have affected his ability to make the transition to the realm he was destined for. Although he desired death, there may in fact have been something on this realm which he was unable to detach from – perhaps a worry or emotional attachment of some kind, which hindered his psychological ability to let go and pass on. Or perhaps he didn't believe in life after death and refused to accept the fact that although he was dead, he was actually still alive.

Alternatively, he could have been resident on another realm, but still harboured an attachment to this realm – perhaps anger at something which had happened to him here – which prompted him to use the ouija board as a conduit for exerting influence here, venting his spleen on the hapless residents of what could have been his former home. Or perhaps he was just a very unpleasant person who grabbed the opportunity of causing suffering to innocent people that the ouija board gave him – the fact that he had lived in the area, perhaps giving him the connection he needed to wield power on this realm.

In either case, the exorcism helped him to move on – either to leave this realm and become resident on another, or to cease his desire or ability to exert malefic influence here, or both.

Likewise the sinister presence in the hotel room could have been an intelligence resident on another realm who was hell-bent on disrupting the spiritual work I was involved with, or could have been an unhappy, bitter, lingering discarnate who hadn't managed to make the full transition from this realm to the next. Either way, I have little doubt that the huge Native American guide set him straight, which would have helped him tremendously.

That's the strange thing about exorcisms which is often overlooked. People only tend to sympathise with the unfortunate people who get scared or pestered by interfering entities, but even more tragic are the discarnates causing the trouble. An exorcism actually helps them to move on to where they should be, and to end pointless attachments, grievances, or malicious activities which are bringing them negative karma. This makes performing an exorcism fantastically worthwhile – and any skilled psychic who does this kind of work on a regular basis has my deepest respect. It is unpleasant, draining, difficult – and can be dangerous, especially if performed by someone without sufficiently advanced psychic abilities.

I do not believe that mediums visiting haunted buildings or performing exorcisms should be filmed purely for entertainment – particularly if done in a sensationalist manner focusing to a large extent on fear.

Many discarnates who cause fear in the living have no malevolent intentions whatsoever. They are just very confused and desperately need help – often leading bizarrely repetitive existences for centuries, or perpetually puzzled as to why no one (except a clairvoyant) can see them.

This kind of vulnerability was brought home to me very forcibly when I was asked to do an exorcism in a building which had formerly been a Roman Catholic church social club. The building, which was in a very poor state of repair, had just been sold and a lot of building work was going on there.

The work, however, suddenly stopped when the builders became too afraid to go down into the basement. These were big, tough Irish guys – not fanciful, dreamy types – but they absolutely refused to go down and carry on working. I was asked to perform an exorcism.

It wasn't made clear what kind of entity it was, or what its intentions were. The builders weren't clairvoyant or clairaudient, so no specific details had been reported. All I knew was that there had been strange noises and an atmosphere which had somehow frightened them.

Since this was a building which was destined to be put to an extremely spiritual use, I suspected the worst: that some malicious entity had made it their mission to cause as much trouble as they could.

I walked down the dark steps with "all guns blazing" – as though marching into battle. As my assistant chanted mantra, I began to summon the help of higher forces. I tuned in and scanned the room clairvoyantly.

To my complete astonishment all I could see was a little old priest in black robes, shivering with terror as he cowered in a corner.

This was no malevolent lower astral force – this was an ordinary, orthodox man who didn't know what was going on. He was probably worried about how the changes being made to the building would affect his "life". I don't know how long he'd been there, or exactly why he was there – perhaps he had died there, or just been very attached to the building – but what was very clear was that he had failed to pass on to the realm he was supposed to be on.

Several guides came onto the scene and whisked him away – no doubt with the intention of helping him make the transition he had been unable to make on his own.

The strange noises and bad vibe (which had probably been caused by the priest's fear and confusion, rather than a desire to do harm) stopped and the builders resumed their work.

In some cases, not only does the intelligence not mean any harm, but they are actually trying, misguidedly, to do good.

"It's an evil spirit! The devil's got her! She's possessed!" This is what I was told by a very distressed single mother whose daughter wouldn't leave the house. She asked me to come and sort her out.

Of course the idea that "the devil had got her" was absurd. If there were such a thing as a supreme lord of evil, which of course there isn't, then I'm sure they would have better, or, rather, worse, things to be doing with their time than pestering young women.

But this was a religious lady from an orthodox background, so she didn't understand exactly what was going on. Nevertheless she was in fact right in thinking her daughter, who was in her teens or early twenties at the time, had indeed been possessed.

Possession is little understood, but is a source of gory fascination even today – glamorised by horror films, dismissed as nonsense by mainstream "science", and feared by orthodox religionists. Put simply, it is when someone is invisibly controlled by a malicious or misguided discarnate. It is not something that most people need to worry about, it's extremely unlikely to happen to you. Generally speaking, possession only happens to someone who is passive enough to accept the state and who has messed with something they shouldn't, though this is not the case here, as far as I know. Serious drug abuse or, more likely, amateur meddling with the "dark arts" can act as triggers. It has also been known for possession to occur in someone who has made a well-intentioned, but hopelessly incompetent, attempt at an exorcism.

I went round to their house and sat down in the front room with the girl while her mother put the kettle on. She seemed very shy and hardly said anything. It was her mother who thought she was possessed – I don't think she did. She hadn't been violent or done anything outlandish. Quite the reverse. She had become increasingly withdrawn and was refusing to leave the house.

Of course mild symptoms like that could purely be due to

psychological reasons and have nothing to do with possession. But I tuned in and saw that this was not the case here. Perhaps her mother, even though she didn't understand what possession really was, had nevertheless realised intuitively that an exorcism was required.

I became aware of a middle-aged Caribbean man wearing a straw hat and the situation unravelled in my mind. I'm not sure how – perhaps intuitively, or perhaps my guides told me.

The man was her father – and he had been "possessing" her because for some reason he didn't want her to meet a man she might marry.

Such a high degree of paternal control is clearly inappropriate – more inappropriate in fact even than if he had behaved in the same way while he was alive. He didn't like the fact that I was there, but my guides explained a few things to him, and he seemed to understand what they were saying and agree that he had been wrong – a realisation which presumably enabled him to pass on in the proper way.

And sure enough, the girl started going out again and leading a normal life.

The saddest exorcism I have ever been involved in resulted, I believe, in the release of discarnates who, again, had no evil intent, they just hadn't let go of the ties of their last incarnation.

My wife and I were on holiday with two close friends in Sicily. A short break – as rare as it was welcome – from our hectic lives. We were staying in a beautiful hotel which had formerly been a monastery. It was idyllically situated in beautiful Mediterranean countryside overlooking the sea. It was one of the best hotels I've ever stayed in and we had a wonderful week there.

Until the last night.

At dusk, the evening before we were due to leave, one of my friends, a lady with many spiritual interests, suggested that the two of us did mantra – sacred chanting – in the beautiful twilit cloisters. Why not?

We chanted for a few minutes, drawing spiritual energy through ourselves and sending it out to the world around us, after which we felt fresh, inspired and invigorated, as you do after most spiritual practices, particularly if done in such sacred surroundings. The four of us then went to dinner, as usual, and had a very pleasant evening.

It was only when I went to bed that I realised something was wrong. I became intensely aware of an almost overwhelming grief. It was probably one of the saddest moments of my life – with no apparent cause. It was as though the building itself was weeping into the sea.

Gradually it became apparent that the grief was in fact coming from a group of monks who had lived there when it was an active monastery. They were deeply upset that this formerly consecrated building was being used as a hotel for pleasure-seeking tourists and were trying to keep the building operational as a place of worship at night by continuing their religious activities there.

The reason I only became aware of this on the last night was because they had been disturbed from their routine by the mantra which my friend and I had been chanting. Not only is mantra a powerful force for healing, which may well have affected their consciousness in some way, stirring some latent desire for change within them, but it also, of course, would seem to them to be a "pagan" ritual, originating as it does from Hinduism and Buddhism – making it a practice which they would not have understood or liked one bit. And the fact that one of these "pagans" was a woman would have added insult to injury – they didn't like the idea of women even staying in "their" monastery, never mind engaging in "heathen" practices.

I got up in the middle of the night and began doing some invocations. I called on my guides for assistance, and as always, being the wonderful people that they are, they wasted no time in responding. Interestingly, two of them on this occasion were intelligences who had been prominent figures in the history of the Roman Catholic Church, one being St Rock about whom I will say more later.

I began to understand what had been going on. The monastery had been very powerful and wealthy in its heyday, exerting tremendous religious and political power over a large part of Sicily. One of its former heads – a senior priest or prior or some such figure – had stayed there for decade after decade as a "ghost", for want of a better word, trying to do much the same as he had done when he was alive. This is not that unusual. What was unusual, however, was that he had used his influence over some of the monks to keep a number of them there as well – perhaps through fear, bullying or the sheer force of his very unpleasant personality. He had the monks running about satisfying his every whim. But, much more seriously, he was holding them up in their journey through evolution.

The arrival of the two guides whom they recognised as revered figures in the Church caused a reaction of awe and excitement throughout the monastery, in fact I do believe that thanks to them some of the monks were released that night.

I also received an apology for the inconvenience caused, and was told by one monk I would be welcome back, provided that I came "without my family". I think this was meant to be a polite way of saying they didn't like the fact that I was sharing a former monk's cell with my wife.

The next morning on my way to breakfast I noticed a portrait on the wall which seemed to be the autocratic prior I had seen in the night. Although the grief which had affected me so much in the night had waned, I was still troubled. I shared the monks' outrage that this holy building was no longer being used as originally intended and was put off the idea of ever staying in a deconsecrated monastery again – something which had never even occurred to me before. It was fortunate that it was the last night of our holiday and not the first!

Now I can see that I should have had more control over my emotions. I should have been aware of the sadness, but also been capable of detaching from it. This is a lesson to me in the importance of developing the strength of character being psychic requires. The more psychic you are, the more prone you are to emotionalism because of all the feelings you become aware of. Failure to control the emotions can potentially be the ruin of even the most talented psychics. Now I almost feel tempted to make a point of staying in a deconsecrated building deliberately in order to practise detachment.

You will notice in all the accounts of exorcisms which I have been involved in (except the first) that all I have really done is act as a link between a specific situation and my guides. They sort the discarnates out, I don't. And in this last incident, it was they who, I believe, helped to release some of the monks – something which would have been completely beyond my capacity without them.

CHAPTER 7

Guides

"There is no being of any race who, if he finds the proper guide,
cannot attain to virtue"
Cicero

The debt I owe to the guides who have helped me over the years cannot be emphasised enough – in terms of both my spiritual and psychic work.

In the early eighties I was contacted by a guide I initially thought was called "Roger". As time went by, however, I realised that his name was in fact "Roch", or "Rock" in English. Because I had never heard of "Roch" – as a person or even as a name – I had conditioned what I was actually told into something which, in my ignorance, I thought made more sense. This is a classic example of how mediums can make mistakes.

He told me a few things about himself, including the fact that he had been involved in healing the plague while he was alive on this realm and had a connection with France and Italy. My wife, who happens to speak Italian, did some research and found that there existed an Italian biography of a man named "San Rocco" ("San" meaning "Saint", "Rocco" being the Italian version of his name), which she read. This confirmed the few things that he had told me, as well as painting a much fuller picture of his remarkable life, though I have subsequently discovered how much accounts of his life differ: even his date of birth is uncertain – varying from 1295 to 1350.

He grew up in Montpellier, France, with the high social status of being the son of the city governor. He emerged from the womb with a red cross on his chest, which was presumably some kind of birthmark, but perhaps also an indication of his unusual destiny.

When he was about twenty his father passed away. St Rock distributed his inherited wealth to the poor, passed governorship of Montpellier to his uncle and set off dressed as a pilgrim for Italy, which was suffering an epidemic of the plague.

Travelling from place to place, he tended the plague's tragic victims, demonstrating his miraculous powers of healing – curing many by making the sign of the cross. However at Piacenza, he himself caught the plague and went off to live in a forest, presumably to die.

Which he probably would have done, had he not been looked after by a remarkable dog who brought him food and licked his sores. The dog belonged to a nobleman called Gothard, who discovered him in the forest by following the unusual animal, and proceeded to become his acolyte. St Rock recovered – and proceeded to continue his healing work, curing not just people, but cattle as well.

When he returned to Montpellier, he was thrown in jail by the governor, possibly his own uncle, on suspicion of being a spy. He stayed there until his death five years later, whereupon his identity was revealed by the strange cross on his chest, and by a document he had with him.

I felt his presence become stronger when The Aetherius Society began a major campaign to get natural healing on the National Health Service. In fact, I believe that it was our healing work that initially attracted him to me and others at the Society. The term "natural healing" included homeopathy, reflexology, acupuncture and other similar techniques, which were much more controversial in the early eighties than they are today. Most significantly, however, as far as I was concerned, it included *spiritual* healing – probably the most controversial of them all.

Dr King was always an ardent supporter of spiritual healing, long before most people even knew what it was, let alone believed it could work. In fact he had been working on psychic research into spiritual healing even before he founded The Aetherius Society in 1955. He always championed the concept that everyone could heal, and was in the fifties and sixties almost a "lone voice" in this respect.

In 1976 he published a groundbreaking book called *You Too Can Heal*. Looking at today's new age movement with its many *reiki* teachers and healers of different kinds who have learnt their skills from scratch, it is hard to believe how radical this message was back in the seventies – even among believers and practitioners. The dogma of the day was that you either had the gift or you didn't, and that to say otherwise was just plain irresponsible.

The *King Technique* is based on a yogic understanding of how the aura (the subtle counterpart to the physical body) and chakras (the "floodgates" in the aura) can be affected by *prana*, or "universal life force" (see Chapter 12), which is invoked and passed into the patient by the healer through visualisation. The healer lays their hands on certain chakras, and on, or near, the area affected by the patient's condition. Full techniques for healing by touch and over a distance, as well as self-healing, are described in detail in my book *The Magic of Healing*, which contains almost the entire content of *You Too Can Heal*, as well as additional material. Again, I am recommending this book not because I wrote it (all royalties go towards the work of The

Aetherius Society), but because it contains Dr King's revolutionary healing techniques which, from experience, I and countless others have found to be so effective.

The campaign ended by us presenting a petition with over 73,000 signatures to 10 Downing Street – which directly or indirectly has yielded positive results. Spiritual healing and other natural treatments are now more accessible through the National Health Service – no doubt to the delight of St Rock and others on the higher realms who are eager to make all forms of healing more widely available.

He is an amazing person, as you can see from his life story, and I feel privileged to have been in contact with him. His messages are gentle, loving and imbued with a deep spiritual sincerity. They offer encouragement, guidance and support, but are not metaphysical treatises – they are more *heart* than *mind*, as it were. His initial contacts were not made because he had a particular interest in me as an individual. He is not *my* guide *per se*, he is *a* guide who helps me – and doubtless many others as well. There is a subtle but important difference.

Ordinary, pleasant people who are not involved in any spiritual work may, when they die, become guardian angels who look after similarly ordinary, pleasant people who are still alive. The identity of the individual the guardian angel picks may be determined by the relationship they had with the person while on this realm. A man may, for example, choose to become his wife's guardian angel after he dies. She may be completely unaware of this, but he can nevertheless help her in unseen ways, a bit like the earlier story of the man whose hands were mysteriously nudged while driving, which saved his life, or the parachutist told to check his pack.

A more advanced discarnate, residing on a higher realm, may choose to become the guide of someone who is on the spiritual path, because they particularly want to help that person in their own spiritual development. Or, as is the case with St Rock, they may make contact, because they wish to support the work that the individual is involved with. These guides can also become your firmest friends as well.

In the early nineties I had a contact with a guide of my good friend Brian Keneipp, who was one of Dr King's closest disciples. The guide was a Native American who told me that he had witnessed a great light coming from an area in the region of Arizona and Utah while a Spiritual Mission was taking place under Dr King's direction, which Brian was also involved in. He had seen that Dr King was in frail health, and that Brian was one of the people who gave him regular healing, so he had decided to assist Brian in healing Dr King, who he was deeply impressed by. I told Brian about this, and he in turn told Dr King who went further than me and actually got the name of the guide: White Deer.

Brian later gained rapport with the guide himself. Even recently another medium also saw this guide with Brian – even though Dr King passed on ten years ago. This illustrates that a guide can be inspired to help an individual because of a particular project they are engaged in, and then continue to support them even after that specific project is completed. This type of guide can become even closer to you than those who were attracted to you for purely personal reasons.

One of the most unusual cases of guides being interested only in a particular project occurred in a small town called Wollongong in Australia. I was staying in Sydney with a friend of mine, Christine, and her family while I was on tour promoting the truth about UFOs. In our youthful zealousness, we had created a publicity schedule which was so hectic as to be almost unworkable – particularly the day we had set aside for Wollongong, a place neither of us were very familiar with, where we had arranged to cram in a radio interview, a TV interview, a newspaper interview and an evening lecture.

The radio interview went extremely well. We were inundated with calls and I came out feeling very satisfied – though a little concerned about how to cope with everything that was coming next.

But unexpected help was at hand: Christine and I were greeted in the reception area by an ordinary-looking, middle-aged woman who had heard the show and driven over to meet us.

"Hi, you must be Richard. Listen, I've got a car and my guides have told me to help you in any way I can today, so anywhere you wanna go, I'm happy to drive you there."

Not nearly as surprised by this as perhaps I should have been, I accepted her kind offer and off we went, while Christine went to check out the hall.

What did surprise us, however, was what happened at the end of the day. Just before the lecture was due to start, I thanked her for all her help and offered her a complimentary ticket to attend the lecture – it was the least I could do after everything she'd done for us.

"Erm, no, no, not for me thanks. I'll leave if you're sure there's nothing else I can help with."

"Well, no, there's nothing else for you to help us with... but are you sure you won't stay?" I asked, a bit puzzled.

"Oh, I'm not into this kind of stuff at all. It's my guides. I don't even agree with a lot of what you say, but I know they do... my guides, that is, and that's why they asked me to come and help."

It seemed unbelievable, but off she went, and I never saw her again. She must have been an exceptionally disciplined medium, in that not only was she able to receive an instruction she didn't agree with, but she also was willing to act upon it without question.

* * *

While it is true that the majority of "my" guides are interested in the work first and foremost, there is one in particular who does show a personal interest in me, though this is also primarily because of the work I am doing. A person and their work can never be separated. Some people say "You are what you eat", others say "You are what you think" – but my philosophy is very much "You are what you do".

This guide, who is a Tibetan lama, is highly respected on the higher realms. I certainly don't flatter myself that I am his only concern. My contact with him is irregular and I have no doubt that he has many other "protégés", for want of a better term, involved in different work on this realm and others.

When I was giving readings in the eighties, I was often helped by two guides who I knew were students, or "*chelas*", of the same spiritual teacher, but I didn't know who the teacher was.

In September 1987 I was given a very important spiritual Initiation by Dr King, the details of which I won't go into. I felt unworthy – and still do – of the great honour he bestowed upon me. In fact when he offered it to me, I at first declined on grounds of inadequacy. That might sound humble, but it didn't please him at all. He wasn't looking for humility – he was looking for people to rise to their calling.

Hearing the disappointed tone of his reaction, I thought hard about what I should do, and resolved to go back to him saying that because I was unworthy, I should make sufficient effort within myself to become worthy – and I am still working on it.

The following year I made a big effort to step up my spiritual practices, in an effort to live up to what had been given to me. That summer one of the two *chelas* got in touch saying that someone quite important – who turned out to be this Tibetan Lama – would like to make contact. I felt that it was only subsequent to the Initiation that such a contact had become possible for me.

They arranged a time for the contact to take place. I prepared myself with some deep breathing exercises and waited.

He told me who he was and some details of his life. He has requested that his identity should not be revealed in this book. I checked the details and found them to be correct, but I also wanted to know more about him.

After considerable research, long before the ease of amazon.com, I found myself calling a publisher in America which I thought might know where I could get hold of a particular biography. They told me that they only knew of one copy on sale in Europe, which was in a place in Scotland – hundreds of miles away.

Within hours, I was called by the son of an elderly friend I was due to visit in Scotland. To my inordinate surprise, he told me that he had arranged for me to visit the premises where the book was located, even though I had not mentioned any of this to him. He knew nothing about my contact, making the synchronicity, as far as I was concerned, quite remarkable.

I went to Scotland, bought the book, and read with fascination the life of an exceptional spiritual individual.

Subsequent contacts with him were always made by appointment through one of the two *chelas*. The times I was given were always convenient, and always just after I had been doing some kind of spiritual activity, like leading a group reciting mantra. Curiously, even when I received a message from him in my office, there was never any interruption: the phone never rang and no one ever knocked on the door.

Since we have become more familiar with each other, the two *chelas* are no longer required as intermediaries, though I still occasionally feel their presence. I think one of the reasons he has chosen to help me is because of the message of the importance of service to others which is the cornerstone of Aetherius Society beliefs. Perhaps he feels he neglected to spread this message sufficiently while he was incarnate, concentrating instead on teaching a wonderful path of personal spiritual development, at which he is an undisputed expert.

He has been very good to me over the years – offering both praise and criticism at appropriate junctures. He has criticised my lack of humility, and urged me to take my own spiritual development more seriously. He also once told me off for not being devotional enough to my Master, Dr King. This is one of the tests of a good personal guide: they will offer constructive criticism as well as encouragement.

* * *

Guidance from higher sources has touched the lives of an eclectic miscellany of individuals throughout history. Those who persist in disbelieving in such guidance, or who regard it as being limited to the lives of fortune-tellers or to quaint fairytales, should be reminded that the great Socrates, father of Western philosophy, genius at logical debate, claimed to have had some kind of guide called a "*daimon*" (not "demon"), on whom he relied for advice.

It is perhaps unsurprising that religious people might be more susceptible to higher guidance than those leading more worldly lives would be. Three Christian saints stand out as remarkable examples of this: St Joan of Arc, St Francis of Assisi, and St Teresa of Ávila. In Roman Catholic dogma communication with the deceased was (and still is) taboo, but communication with saints and angels, was, if accepted as genuine, regarded as miraculous – if not accepted, as heresy.

St Joan was born at Domrémy in Champagne, France, in 1412. Her mother was kind and loving, her father, a peasant farmer, was a good man, but somewhat morose. The family was poor, but not on the breadline. Women of her class at that time would have been illiterate, but she was good at the things that would have been considered important to a young girl, such as sewing and spinning. She was also mature beyond her years – pious, compassionate, serious and accustomed to absorbing herself in prayer.

She had her first clairaudient experience when she was just 13. She heard a voice which sounded as though it came from someone speaking quite close to her – but all she could see was bright light. Later she could actually see the "people" who spoke to her, recognising them as, among others, St Michael, St Catherine, and St Margaret. No one knows how she recognised them. She refused to describe them. The only thing she made clear was that she had seen them with her own eyes, as clearly as if she was looking at anyone else.

It seems that her mission was only revealed to her gradually. Let me be clear that I am neither endorsing nor criticising this mission – only using it as an illustration of the influence guides can have in the life of a dedicated clairaudient.

When she was just 16, her voices instructed her to go to see a commandant called Robert Baudricot, who was resident in the nearby town of Vaucouleurs. However, she received a brusque reception and was sent home, which is hardly surprising; even the kindest of soldiers are, after all, unlikely to pay much heed to a 16-year-old girl who says she's been hearing voices.

As the military situation in France worsened, Joan's voices became more insistent. She resisted, wondering what a poor young girl could possibly hope to achieve, but eventually she gave in and went back to Vaucouleurs the following year. This time she stayed in the town, despite Baudricot's understandable scepticism. Her piety and quiet persistence made him more inclined to take her seriously, but what really made an impression was when her report that a grave defeat had been suffered in the Battle of Herrings was later confirmed to be true.

Following this she was allowed to go to Chinon, accompanied by men-at-arms, to see Charles VII – the uncrowned King. She dressed as a man and slept in her clothes, presumably to avoid anything remotely improper befalling her. When she reached Chinon, Charles had decided to test her by hiding among his courtiers to see if she could recognise him – which she immediately did. She told him she wanted to fight the English and that he would be crowned at Reims.

There was strong opposition to this foolhardy madwoman, as they saw her, at court, but Joan was given a sign by her voices, which she revealed only to Charles. This got her through to the next round:

interrogation by theologians and bishops at Poitiers, who were impressed by her simple sincerity, but failed to state definitely whether or not they thought her genuine, which is perhaps only to be expected in view of the widespread fear of heresy at the time. Nevertheless, in view of the dire plight of the King's cause, it was decided that it would be a good idea to let her have a go and see what came of it.

She went back to Chinon to prepare. She refused the sword offered her by the King, because her voices had told her that she should use an ancient sword to be found buried in the church of Sainte-Catherine-de-Fierbois – which indeed it was.

Her military success was astounding. With her unique guidance, she had an excellent sense of timing. For example, one evening while resting, she suddenly got up and declared that she should go and attack the English – only to find that she was to arrive on the scene at just the right moment. Later that week the English retreated, but because it was Sunday she would not allow them to be pursued.

In 1429, when Joan was still only 17, Charles was crowned at Reims, just as her voices had said he would be. A few months later the King ennobled her and her family.

However, the fighting continued, and her voices told her that she would be taken prisoner, which indeed she was, by a soldier in the service of John of Luxemburg. She was later sold for a great deal of money to the English, who in collusion with her French enemies put her on trial for heresy – an easy thing for them to do considering the grandeur of her claims. The seriousness of this charge, and the fact that she wore men's clothing, meant she was forbidden from attending Mass while in prison. At one point she was even confined in an iron cage, with chains on her hands, feet and neck – on account of her having tried to escape.

Joan was burnt at the stake in 1431, still only a teenager. Her courage as inspiring as her fate tragic, today she is remembered more for her victory over the prejudices against her age, gender and social class, than for her military achievements. Personally I regard her first and foremost as being a great martyr for clairaudience.

Moving though her story is, I'm glad to say that the cases of St Teresa and St Francis, though not without hardship, are considerably more cheerful.

St Teresa was born in 1515 to a good family in Ávila, Spain. Pretty, intelligent, impulsive, romantic, emotional, saintly, fun, self-critical, but perhaps most of all determined – she was clearly a girl who would never allow mediocrity to cloud her radiant destiny. When she was only about six she persuaded her older brother Rodrigo to go with her to the land of the Moors, so they could get their heads cut off, not so much for the glory of God, but in order to get to Heaven as quickly as possible. Fortunately they were intercepted by an uncle before they'd got very far. Religious fervour of this degree at such a young age could either be taken as a sign of phenomenal piety, or as a sign of a larger-than-life personality: probably it was a bit of both.

As a teenager she became interested in things she later came to regard as sinful like wearing perfume, spending time on her hair and socialising with her worldly-minded cousins. But things changed somewhat when, on account of her having no older sister or mother (who had not long since passed away) to exert virtuous womanly influence on her, she was sent to a convent and put in the temporary care of Augustinian nuns.

After a while, under the influence of her devout Uncle, she decided to become a nun herself – which, strange though it may sound considering he had sent her to a convent – her father refused to consent to. However this wasn't going to stop a girl like Teresa: she and her younger brother Antonio ran away together to begin new lives of spiritual devotion. At the age of about 21 she joined the Carmelite Monastery of the Incarnation of Ávila.

The convent was quite lax. Wealth seemed to be valued more than virtue. Many of the nuns wore jewellery and attractive clothing – some even had servants. She was encouraged to have visitors, because of the gifts they brought. The lack of serious religious discipline lead her into various worldly "temptations" which her tender conscience rebuked her bitterly for. She even stopped praying because she thought herself too dreadful a sinner to have such intimate contact with the Almighty.

When she was eventually persuaded to resume her devotions, she found it extremely hard to concentrate, and even wondered what penance she wouldn't rather have undergone instead of having to pray.

But she was to be rewarded for the impassioned stamina she demonstrated in her desire to lead a truly spiritual life. She began to have all kinds of mystical experiences, including visions and hearing voices – something one would have thought would be celebrated, but, all too predictably, it was all put down to being the work of the devil. She was even instructed to point scornfully whenever she had a vision, which of course she was loathe to do, but obeyed nevertheless. Worse still, she was forbidden from praying. However, she found it impossible to accept that experiences which made her feel so inspired could possibly be anything but the work of God.

When she resolved to start her own convent – St Joseph's – based on the ideals of poverty and prayer, her plan was met with staunch opposition, but true to form she proceeded nevertheless. In fact it turned out to be the first of many. She also put pen to paper, describing her mystical experiences and thoughts, lacing her writing with the excessive humility which was one of the idiosyncrasies that defined her complex character – even in the first paragraph of her autobiography we find the harshly self-condemning words: "If I had not been so wicked".

Her experiences are extraordinary. She levitated, she saw angels, but most interestingly of all she became filled with an intense love for God. Immortalised by Gian Lorenzo Bernini's marble sculpture, *The Ecstasy of St Teresa*, she records seeing an angel, on her left, as an apparently physical manifestation. This even she regarded as unusual, in that, although she often saw angels – they were usually only as "intellectual visions". On the small side, but very beautiful, she wondered if he was a cherub.

He was holding a golden spear, on the end of which it looked as though there was some kind of fire. He thrust it into her heart, leaving her feeling filled with Divine love. She described it as a pain, both spiritual and physical, which, strange though it sounds, caused her to experience a kind of bliss. To someone versed in yoga philosophy, this sounds like a description of the power of Kundalini, which I will talk more about in Chapter 10, being risen, at least partially, to the heart chakra.

St Francis never had an experience quite like this – not that we know of at least – but he is in some ways similar to St Teresa. Had they not lived 300 years apart, I am sure they would have got on very well.

He was born in the Italian city of Assisi in 1181 or 82. His father, Peter Bernadone, was a rich merchant and his mother, Pica, is thought to have been a noblewoman from Provence. He was indulged by his parents, and not in any way studious. But the young Francis had other qualities: he was handsome, fun-loving, well-mannered, well-dressed, and witty – all of which, combined with his extravagance and general worldliness, served to make him extremely popular.

No one could have suspected what was coming.

This lad's lad, this embodiment of "cool", this personification of frivolous boyishness, was to become one of the most celebrated saints of all time. Perhaps in addition to being Patron Saint of Italy and ecology, he should be made Patron Saint of parents who worry what will become of their troublesome teenage sons.

At the age of around 20, Francis joined the men of the town to go and fight the Perugians. He was taken prisoner and held in Perugia for over a year, where he became ill. His mind, deprived of its usual diversions, turned inwards and he began to ponder upon the futility of his way of life.

However, health restored, undeterred by his period of captivity, he resolved to embark upon a career in the military – a fitting vocation for a man of his disposition. The night before he left for the Neapolitan States to fight against the emperor, he had a dream in which he saw a large hall full of armour marked with the Cross. A voice told him it was for him and his soldiers, which he took to be a sign that he would become a great prince.

He fell ill once again at a place called Spoleto. And once again illness proved to play a key role in his spiritual awakening. He had another dream – a voice told him to head back for Assisi, which he did.

He didn't change overnight. Back in his hometown he still joined in the fun and games of his old friends, but with less enthusiasm. He gradually gave up his extravagant lifestyle and sought to confirm his calling through prayer and solitude.

He also sought to cultivate an active sense of charity and humility within himself. One day out on horseback he came across a leper, from whom he instinctively recoiled. But, on reflection, he decided to get down from his horse, and give him alms. In fact he purportedly even kissed his hand – quite a feat considering he had always been deeply repulsed by lepers. He also went on a pilgrimage to Rome, where he emptied his purse on the tomb of St Peter – so profoundly unimpressed was he at the pitiful offerings he saw there. He then swapped clothes with a beggar, and stood fasting by the door of the basilica for the remainder of the day.

It seems that his first experience which was truly clairaudient (in that it happened to him while he was awake and not in a dream) occurred shortly after his return to Assisi in an old chapel, San Damiano, outside of town. As he was praying he heard a voice instructing him to "repair my house". Francis interpreted this literally as referring to the near derelict chapel he was in at the time. He got some good-quality cloth from his father's shop and rode to Foligno, where he sold not only the cloth, but the horse as well. However the priest at St Damiano's refused to accept his money. Francis was so annoyed he flung the money out of the window.

His father was furious at this outlandish behaviour – so much so in fact that Francis hid in a cave near the chapel for several weeks. When he eventually emerged, in an extremely bedraggled state, his father beat him and locked him in a closet. His mother released him, but his father soon caught up with him. He was brought before the Bishop of Assisi, in front of whom Francis stripped naked. He gave his clothes to his father and announced, in a polite but definite way that God was to be his father from then on. The Bishop was understandably somewhat taken aback and gave him something to wear, after which the newly-fledged ascetic disappeared into the countryside.

He began preaching as an unlicensed layperson, but when he'd gathered together a dozen followers had the good sense to go to Rome to seek approval from Pope Innocent III, which was indeed given, despite initial hesitation, after the Pope had an inspired dream indicating what decision he should make.

The Franciscan order was officially founded – and it grew rapidly.

His remarkable dedication to following Jesus's example of poverty and love, yielded a miracle which happened several years later. He had an angelic vision, after which he was left permanently marked with "stigmata" (scars representing those of crucifixion).

He died in his 40s, in 1226, and was canonized less than two years later – in contrast to St Teresa who had to wait 40 years before she was canonized, and St Joan who had to wait almost 500 years.

The exact nature of the experiences of these three saints is hard to pin down. Interpreted and recorded in line with the dogma of the time, it is unlikely we will ever have any idea, for example, exactly what kind of intelligence the "angel" who "stabbed" St Teresa was. Nor will we ever know if St Joan was right about the identity of her voices. Nor indeed the identity of St Francis's inspiration. But what is very clear is that some kind of guidance was at work   forces with a religious agenda using people as instruments to perform certain jobs, bringing about remarkable results.

* * *

Higher guidance takes different forms for different people at different times. That it has not been banished to the distant past, or indeed segregated to a religious, spiritual or philosophical domain, is demonstrated by its appearance in the oddest place of all: British and American politics.

It is little known that Winston Churchill (1874-1965) is said to have had psychic abilities – abilities which even saved his life. When he escaped from the Boers in Pretoria in the Boer War, he leapt from a train in a place totally unfamiliar to him. He didn't know who he could trust or where to turn, but, miraculously, ended up finding the one house in the whole region which was pro-British.

Many years later, during the London blitz he was mysteriously "told" to sit in the right-hand seat of the car he was travelling in instead of the left, which is where he normally sat. Sure enough a bomb fell not far from the vehicle, which, had he not been sitting where he was, would have turned over. Other instances include a premonition in which he "saw" a large kitchen window at Downing Street being shattered. All the staff were ordered to go to the shelter. A few minutes later a bomb fell causing the kitchen to be destroyed. In his latter years, he even saw his late father, Lord Randolph Churchill who had been Chancellor of the Exchequer, and chatted to him about politics.

Abraham Lincoln (1809-1865) reportedly had premonitions

which came to him in dreams, among them one regarding his own assassination. He also had an interest in Spiritualism. Medium Nettie Colburn Maynard records the fact that the President knew many mediums and sought counsel from "the other side" on matters of great importance. Nettie herself, whose mediumistic powers were evident from an early age, was able to enter a trance and allow guides to speak through her at length to the President and his wife – giving specific information and advice.

* * *

It is a fine line between receiving guidance from the other realms and channelling. Broadly speaking channelling is associated with receiving longer, more precise communications, whereas receiving guidance might be the odd sentence of advice or encouragement here and there, or even just a feeling. Channelling is of course more difficult, and consequently less common, and its results very different…

CHAPTER 8

Messages

"The communication
Of the dead is tongued with fire beyond the language of the living"
T. S. Eliot

A harvest moon, oh how it shines upon the darkened, glowering masses beneath it. A twilight sun, so warm it welcomes all humanity to gaze upon it. A trickle of rain, so light it refreshes those who accept nature's cleansing droplets. And yet all too often the moonlit streets are not trod by those who inhabit the shadows. They turn their backs upon the warmth of the twilight sun. They protect themselves from the cleansing shower which nature has provided. I did not realise then that all is there for the waiting ones, while nothing exists for those who refuse to see it.

I know it now. I know it now, for I have communed with those who understand the laws of nature, God's laws. A blight has descended upon the people and they have turned their faces heavenwards, but all they see is clouds. I have faith in the human spirit, but I see too little of it. Here we share a common bond for we know that death is an illusion. There death is everywhere to behold. A sinking feeling is upon them – needlessly so, needlessly so, my friends.

So upwards look beyond the clouds of doubt and despair into the light beyond. And then will the moon lighten your path, the sun warm you on your journey and the rain cleanse you when you are wearied by the load. The clouds will part and you will be refreshed and your vision no longer impaired for all that lies before you will be free of the doubts and despair which had beset you. That is the message I wish to convey for I have changed since my time down there. Thanks be to God.

This is a piece I recently channelled from a writer I believe to have been Russian who was not religious at all while he was on this realm.

His outlook has changed in a distinctly spiritual direction since his passing, exemplified by his reference to "...the laws of nature, God's laws...". Religion and spirituality are of course the same thing on the higher realms, because religion is not tainted by the dogmatism, corruption, bloodshed and repression which are so rife on this realm, and the realms below this. To an advanced person the higher realms are truly wonderful places to be – and the higher you go the more wonderful they become. However, as a general rule, because this realm is the best place to gain experience, and, more importantly, to make a real difference to the world as a whole, many of those on the higher realms are anxious to return here. This is one of the signs of their spiritual advancement.

Another former atheist who has contacted me from the higher realms is Charles Bradlaugh. In fact he wasn't even just an atheist, he was the founder of the National Secular Society, which in 1866, when the society started, must have seemed very radical indeed.

Born in 1833, he briefly joined the army in his late teens before following his father into the lower echelons of the law. He then became a popular antireligious lecturer, publicly challenging the authority of the Bible with believers – often at great length.

He was elected MP for Northampton in 1880, but was not

allowed to take his seat because he objected to the religious oath which Members of Parliament were required to take at that time. He was re-elected three times, and in January 1886, eventually allowed to make a non-religious affirmation.

He was an outspoken supporter of contraception as a weapon against poverty, at a time when both the Church of England and the Roman Catholic Church were vigorously opposed to it. During the 1870s and 1880s he was a close associate of the great humanitarian and brilliant orator Annie Besant (1847-1933) – both of them similarly radical and courageous in their pioneering campaign for reform.

However they ended up going down very different paths. While he remained an atheist until his death in 1891, in 1889 Annie Besant became a Theosophist – "Theosophy", meaning "Divine Wisdom" – and went on to write a number of profound treatises on metaphysics and occultism.

In the late eighties I received a message from someone on the higher realms who introduced himself initially as "The Libertarian", and then mysteriously signed off as "The C.B. Network". Before mobile phones were around, "CB Radios" were used a lot for short distance wireless communication, and I thought that getting the phrase "C.B. Network" from another realm was a kind of joke – because, serious though they are in their work, people on the higher realms do still make jokes and often have a great sense of humour. Eventually, however, I got the full name – "The Charles Bradlaugh Network" – which meant nothing to me at the time. As had happened with St Rock and the Lama, Mr Bradlaugh told me a few salient details about his life, which I checked and found to be correct.

Just as when he was alive, he is engaged in very useful pioneering work on the other realms. He organises a wide network, including writers, musicians, politicians, artists, and religious figures, probably mainly Western, who help to inspire the physical realm. They don't all work together all the time – but he is able to get in touch with them when necessary and request that they help with a specific project which could benefit from their skill or influence. After I had been told about his Network, I discovered that Annie Besant, who, as well as being a great philanthropist, was a brilliant psychic, had said something similar about him. She hadn't described it as a network as such, but had said that he was "labouring to inspire statesmen and speakers with high ideals and useful lines of work." (p.155 *Popular Lectures on Theosophy*, second edition, 1912, Annie Besant, published by The Theosophist Office, Adyar, Madras, India)

But, unlike when he was alive, he is far from being an atheist – in fact he is an ardent believer, not in conventional dogma of course, but in deep spiritual truths. He also has the deepest respect for Dr George King, which is probably one of the main reasons he contacted me. Dr King was far too busy to receive such a contact himself and, as I am sure Charles Bradlaugh would be the first to agree, of much too high a calibre to channel even inspired guides from the other realms.

In early January 2006 I received a message from him, entitled 'A New Year Exhortation', of which the following is an extract.

Today presents so many new opportunities. It matters not in the end whether you are recognised in the world, because you will be in the hereafter. Just as so many who have prospered in the world have declined into insignificance at the instant they passed over. What counts is deeds, results, improvements and help – those are the badges of merit we all should wear.

My call to arms is not new, and very unoriginal, but I make it for this reason. When you join us here, on the other side, and look back upon your life, it will be moments of heroism that you seek to find, not moments of success; sacrifices you made, not recognition you received; differences you made to others, not their appreciation or even love for you. Seek these things out here and now, and then later the rewards will come. Believe me, I know. I missed many such opportunities and grasped but few!

Now I wait in line for a chance to put my record straight, to clean my slate and receive the only reward any of us truly crave – though we often forget it – namely peace with our inner selves. You can't find peace and have a guilty conscience at the same time. You can mask your guilt behind earthly power and status, but it will emerge again, of that you can be sure. So, my new year message is: ignore the standards you meet in your world and strive for the standards of the Great Ones. What would Jesus do or Buddha think? What would George King say? Those are surer guides than the hollow lists produced to empower the status quo by government institutions. I challenged such institutions when I last was incarnate. Things have improved since then, in so many ways, and deteriorated in others. The change must come from within the hearts and souls of ordinary people – then they will be the true heroes of this coming year.

Notice how self-critical he is, despite his success and achievements.

I believe that one of the missed opportunities he mentions may refer to the fact that he didn't join The Theosophical Society like his friend Annie Besant.

It is also interesting that he talks about "hollow lists produced to empower the status quo". The higher realms have no interest whatsoever in empowering the status quo – they wish to bring about spiritual change, not keep things as they are. This is another difference between a communication from an overly-attached guardian angel and a higher guide. A guardian angel who stoops to interfere in petty matters – such as what school the grandchildren should go to, whether or not your husband is going to get promoted, whether your bachelor brother will ever get married etc. – is in effect endorsing life as it is, rather than guiding someone to lead life as it should be led. While the above examples may have their place in many people's lives, they do not compare to the radical vision of the higher realms for improving world conditions. They are matters to be dealt with by the living – not the deceased, whereas spiritual revitalisation is something that everyone – living and deceased – should be working for.

* * *

Nevertheless it is certainly not the case that all material channelled from the other realms is of such a serious nature as the two messages above. Quite the contrary.

It is little known that American actress and sex symbol Mae West (1892/93-1980) was reportedly fascinated by spirituality and psychic phenomena. She attended séances and even did practices – sitting on a straight-backed chair, hands on knees – in order to develop her own psychic abilities.

It would appear either that these practices worked, or that she was already psychic. She was reportedly able to write scripts in just three or four days, dictating while she was apparently in a trance – though it is unclear exactly what is meant by "trance". This was not an unconscious thing – she would actually call upon spirits to assist her, relying on them rather than her own imagination, to formulate the plots of "her" works.

If indeed she was channelling, or at the very least receiving some kind of guidance, which is certainly possible and seems probable, I would have no idea what kind of calibre her guides were. It would be easy to jump to the conclusion that because her work was hardly spiritual in nature, that it came from quite a poor calibre of guide. But neither life – nor death – are that simple. It could perhaps be that it was all part of a plan to combat the repression and hypocrisy which were rife particularly in the early part of her career.

Also in the entertainment industry, Paul McCartney recounted an interesting incident to Barry Miles, his biographer, regarding an apparently inexplicable experience he had had. He woke up one morning in 1965 with a tune in his head. He played it on the piano, using improvised lyrics rhyming "scrambled eggs" with "legs". He loved it – though he had a hard time believing that he had written it himself, which of course, quite possibly he hadn't: it is my belief that he may well have received it from a guide. Today the tune is known as *Yesterday*, and is one of the most successful pop songs of all time.

This type of phenomenon is also recorded in classical music – though unfortunately, again, we can't do more than speculate that a guide, or guides, *may* have been involved. According to his daughter, Carice, British composer Sir Edward Elgar (1857-1934) awoke one morning during a period of ill health and proceeded to jot down the first theme of his Cello Concerto. Robert Schumann (1810-1856), the German Romantic composer, had an interest in Spiritualism, and claimed that he heard the music and voices of angels. He also claimed that he had been visited by the deceased composer Franz Schubert (1797-1828), who had given him a wonderful melody.

Personally, I also wonder if Russian composer Sergey Rachmaninoff (1873-1943) wasn't channelling – either consciously or unconsciously. I have heard that his eyes would be seen to glaze, which could be an indication of entering some kind of trance. It is interesting to note how similar his *Piano Concerto No. 2* is in feeling to the *Piano Concerto No. 1* of Tchaikovsky who had died in 1893. This could of course just be normal musical influence, but it could also perhaps be something more.

Possibly the finest example of poetical channelling is William Blake (1757-1827). The son of a London hosier, he was psychic from childhood; aged nine he told his mother he had seen angels in a tree – which could possibly have been "devas", discussed in Chapter 11. He also saw entities akin to angels in a field where farm labourers were working – and reported seeing The Prophet Ezekiel and other Biblical and historical figures.

When he was ten he went to drawing school, and a few years later became an engraver's apprentice. In 1779 he entered the Royal Academy – but it didn't go well. His art was not understood and he loathed the Academy's president. Following the death of his father, he opened a print shop in 1784, where Robert, his younger brother assisted him. However, it wasn't long before Robert became ill. When he passed away, William actually saw a vision of him rising upwards through the ceiling, in great joy. And a little thing like death wasn't going to stop Robert from helping his brother, just as he had while he had been incarnate. He came to his brother in a dream and described a new technique to him which William called "illuminated printing".

His fortunes waxed and waned throughout his life – though he was never particularly successful in worldly terms. However in 1819, just six years before his death, he found a generous patron, a painter called John Linnell, and became encircled by a group of young artists who afforded him the reverence he deserved.

Many people thought him mad in his own time and it is a poor reflection of our progress, or rather the lack of it, that, while the modern world may concede that he was a genius, the true nature of his abilities and experience is so little understood even today. His patron, who I would imagine knew him better than most, countered any smear of doubt regarding his mental health, saying he never encountered any trace of madness in him.

He claimed that poetry was dictated to him. For example, he claimed that he wrote as many as 30 lines in one go of his epic *Jerusalem* in hardly any time at all. However, in addition to having the ability to channel, I believe that Blake was a poetic genius in his own right, whereas I have virtually no poetical ability whatsoever. I have chosen to publish my own channelled poems primarily to illustrate this particular application of channelling, and also to share the insights contained within the poems into life after death – and indeed life before death.

CHAPTER 9

Poems

"Poets are the hierophants of an unapprehended inspiration"
Percy Bysshe Shelley

Guide: "Hello. It's John Smith here. Got a mo?"

Medium: "Yeah – sure. John Smith... right. So who were you when you were last incarnate?"

Guide: "I was a priest in Wolverhampton who wrote poems about angels."

Medium: "Sounds nice. What realm did you get to for doing that then?"

Guide: "Level three."

Medium: "That's not bad then, is it? Good on you!"

Guide: "It's OK – could be better, could be worse."

Medium: "So I suppose you've got a poem for me."

Guide: "That's right, yes. I did this one while I was on holiday on level four."

Medium: "Level four, eh? That must have been great. Hope you got a good deal."

Guide: "Sure did. I'd saved over 3000 ether miles on my HSBC (Heaven & Shangri-La Banking Corporation) Karma Kard, so I projected there free of charge – and once you're there they're all such lovely folk that they never ask for any money – you don't have to pay for a thing! It's great! Anyway, you got a pen handy, 'cause I'm ready with the poem now?"

Medium: "Yes. Ready. Hope it's a good'un."

Getting a message from a guide is NOTHING like this.

It's just not that easy.

* * *

Until recently only some of the people closest to me knew the full extent of my channelling. I've never kept it a secret, but nor have I gone out of my way to make every detail widely known.

One of the people I used to discuss it with the most was naturally my teacher, Dr King. I was incredibly fortunate to receive guidance from a medium of his brilliance. He was a Master, I am not. He could receive messages from Masters. I cannot. His genius at receiving information from beings on the higher realms and beyond is, I believe, unequalled in human history – making my feeble abilities seem less than paltry by comparison. Likewise the information he received was of world-saving importance – whereas my comparatively insignificant messages are of an immeasurably lower calibre, a fact which my guides would readily agree with.

Some of the mistakes I made in the early days have had a big effect on me – not least in helping me understand how easy it is for mediums to get things wrong. Some people in the new age movement think that any channelled communication which isn't perfect is the result of dark force interference. In fact what is often happening is that the medium is getting something good, but mixing it in with their own ego and imagination – sometimes resulting in a curious mix of the profound and the absurd. This is when it is essential for the medium to listen to, and follow, the guidance of someone who knows better. If they don't, the situation may well get worse.

Even now I am extremely cautious of any claim I make, and I still question everything I get. This is particularly true when it comes to getting a name. The reason I wanted to include that silly little conversation at the start of this chapter was to try to illustrate to non-mediumistic readers that with contacting guides it's not simply a case of "easy if you know how".

I have come to the conclusion that the more specific and unfamiliar the material is to the medium, the harder it is for them to receive it correctly – or at all. Precise names, numbers, and foreign words which are unknown to the medium are very difficult for this reason. Compare it with listening to the radio. Being a medium is like listening to a radio frequency which is very quiet, and has lots of crackly interference. If you were listening to a quiet, crackly radio show, you'd probably be able to get the general gist of what the programme was about, and even hear the odd sentence perfectly clearly, but imagine if it was a show about the history of Mongolia with lots of dates and strange-sounding foreign names. You'd have to concentrate a lot harder even just to get the gist of it, but to get all the names and dates – and be sure that you'd got them right – would be very unlikely indeed.

Nevertheless it is possible to get names – if you are prepared to put in the required time and energy, provided that the communicating intelligence wants you to get their name, which is not always the case. Some of the communications I have received are from guides who do not wish their names to be revealed in this book, such as the Lama discussed in Chapter 7. They may be concerned that making it commonly known that I was in touch with them could in some way jeopardise other work they were involved in. Or they may be concerned that revelation of their identity would be too distracting, or unnecessarily offensive to the establishment. If someone for example were to receive a message from Pope John Paul II (which I haven't, by the way), he or the powers that be on the higher realms may regard revealing this fact as being potentially too confusing to ordinary Roman Catholics. Or they may be worried that the medium would become known first and foremost as "Pope John Paul II's Channel", which could deflect attention from what he was actually trying to achieve.

I would certainly not want to become known as "Such and such a famous person's channel" – even if it was true. One reason, to be honest, is because it can look so tacky when some mediums make such claims. I myself would be sceptical of anyone's claim to be receiving substantial communications from a discarnate celebrity. Everyone would think that such a medium was just cashing in, and, if the person were recently deceased, the media would – in many cases quite justifiably – accuse the medium of being insensitive to the feelings of the surviving friends and relatives.

This book is intended to help people understand what Gods, guides and guardian angels really are – it is not meant to be an entertaining selection of excerpts from dead celebrities.

For these reasons I am not revealing the names of all my communicators. Perhaps the right time will come to reveal a few more names. I know that some people close to me feel that I am being too reticent, and I have no doubt that some of the guides in question would like me to publish their names. But I'm the one on the physical realm – they are not – and they are willing to leave it to me.

The reason I have had contacts with a number of well-known people is our good friend Mr Bradlaugh and his marvellous

Network. As a keen supporter of the work which I am involved in, it is, and has been for some time, his wish to be of whatever assistance he can – and to arrange for other appropriate people to be of assistance as well. One way he has chosen to do this is by working on a project which he believes, among other things, will help to promote the concept of channelling in the correct way; spread the truth about life after death; and spread the inspiring message that people can and often do develop a much deeper spiritual awareness after death.

I do not know if the 'Poetry Project' – as I have nicknamed it, was his concept or not. It involves accomplished, reasonably advanced guides giving me a varied selection of poems, to which this chapter is devoted.

I think one reason that poetry was chosen is that I myself am not a very good poet. What I am about to say may sound strange to non-psychic readers, but the use of poetry as a genre is evidence to *me* that they are channelled. This again goes back to the conversation at the beginning of this chapter. It isn't like that. I don't just hear and know immediately exactly what it is and where it's coming from – though I am aware of the communicator's vibe. I don't question it while it is going on. I'd lose my concentration if I did. But afterwards I sometimes go through a period of doubt. But then again – doubt is surely the parent of certainty.

This process of self-doubt will puzzle people still stuck in the "psychics-know-everything-or-nothing" mindset – and also perhaps be unexpected to psychics who aren't willing to subject themselves to this kind of self-interrogation. Twenty years ago, I wouldn't have been willing either – at least not in the way that I am now. Although it seems paradoxical, I now think that the reason for this is that I was not sure enough of my own abilities to seriously question them.

One thing I am certain of is that I could not have written the following poem on my own in the few minutes it took me:

Journey with no End

Meand'ring through the valley's floor,
A tributary leads to the shore.
And so it is with human thought,
Which leads to all but comes from naught.

A finite ray of God's own light,
Starting dull and ending bright,
An emblem of a future day,
Of life which comes from mortal clay.

And so it shines its radiant beams,
Upon the vast, unwanted dreams
Of reckless men and hopeless fools,
Of vagabonds who shape their tools

From earthy fantasies so bleak
That even loose-tongued knaves won't speak
Of all they want in darkest night –
A sad reflection of their blight.

But tarry not with wretched thought,
For e'en from this can light be brought!
When truth bears down upon its prey,

Your life will turn from night to day!

The ne'er-do-wells become the free,
The tributary leads to the sea,
The ocean's waves absorb the dross –
An alchemy of human loss.

Until it meets infinity,
A fragment of eternity,
A monumental, beauteous sight
When thought's consumed in purest light.

This is the journey with no end,
In comp'ny with God's Timeless Friend:
The soundless sound – the voiceless voice –
The thought at which all men rejoice.

The spirit speaks – the worlds are still –
For 'tis the thing called Divine Will.
And that all started with a thought,
'Pon which God's magic has been wrought.

I felt that this poem was written by two people who had lived in the 16th or 17th century. They may well have had lives since then of course, but this was the period of their experience that they had drawn on to write this poem. An important point to make clear is that just because the poets were alive at that time, and were employing the expertise they had developed and manifested during that period, it doesn't mean that this is a 16th/17th-century poem. The poets are not stuck in a time warp. They are alive on the other realms *now* – and are to a certain extent aware of what is going on here on this realm. Language will no doubt have changed up there, just as it has changed here. Having said that, this poem uses an iambic metre and is written in rhyming couplets, both of which, I have been told since, were commonly used techniques in the seventeenth century. Likewise, terms like "vagabonds", "ne'er-do-wells" and "knaves" were used in that period.

I woke up with the name of one of the poets one morning. I don't know where it had come from – probably he, or another guide, had told me in the night. Or it could have been my intuition, which, after some contemplation, had finally managed to pluck it from the ethers.

Daven… Daven… something beginning with Daven…

Davenport.

Anxious to check this out I looked up "Davenport" in my encyclopaedia, but found nothing that struck a cord. However, after a little more research, I did discover that there had been a 17th-century poet called Sir William Daven*ant* (also spelled D'avenant). I felt that was the name I was looking for.

Davenant lived in troubled times and led a dangerous life. Born in Oxford in 1606, he was in fact Shakespeare's godson – and may even have been his illegitimate son. He was reckless by nature, and a fighter in spirit. These qualities, as well as his literary achievements, got him noticed by Henrietta Maria, wife of King Charles I. He was made poet laureate in 1638.

In 1642 civil war broke out, destroying his plan to build a theatre. A staunch Royalist, the King knighted him in 1643 for having brought supplies across the Channel. After Charles I was executed, Henrietta Maria sent him away to America. He didn't get far, however, before being captured – resulting in his imprisonment in the Tower of London until 1654.

Two years later he tried to resuscitate English drama which had been smothered by Oliver Cromwell, the strict puritan who forbade so many things, including mince pies. He wrote a work which he protected under the dour name of *Declamations and Musick*, which paved the way for his creation of the first public opera in England: *The Siege of Rhodes Made a Representation by the Art of Prospective in Scenes, And the Story sung in Recitative Musick*, in which painted sets and a female actress-singer were seen for the first time on the English public stage. After the Restoration, he founded the new Duke of York's Playhouse in Lincoln's Inn Fields, where plays where written, directed, produced, managed and adapted by him. He died in London in April 1668.

After confirmation from "the other side", I am now confident that he is one of the two authors of *Journey with no End*. The other one, I feel, lived a bit earlier than him. I believe it to be Fulke Greville, Lord Brooke (1554-1628), who was a poet and statesman, and counted Sir Francis Bacon among his friends.

Davenant isn't particularly well regarded as a poet – and he certainly isn't well known today. This doesn't bother him in the least: my impression is that he is indifferent to literary criticism, and happy to do what he does regardless of other people's opinions.

I received it in my office. It is a strange thing that I am never interrupted when receiving a message. The phone never rings and no one ever comes in. But this poem was the exception.

Someone came in briefly and then left. I had just written "This is the journey with no end" in the penultimate stanza. I can't help but wonder if this interruption wasn't in some way significant. That I should be made to stop just after writing down that there is "no end", and then, after a brief pause, start again, thereby enacting the concept of there being no end, strikes me as possibly being an example of synchronicity, perhaps indicating that this is the most important line of the poem, which is one of the reasons I have given it the title of *Journey with no End*. I have had to put the punctuation in afterwards, by the way – that is not something I usually channel.

It starts quietly and pleasantly but then becomes so bleak as to be almost comical, as it describes the worst of humankind ("reckless men", "hopeless fools" and "vagabonds") whose plans and desires are so terrible that even bad-lads prone to gossip ("loose-tongued knaves") can't bear to talk about them.

Just after this I felt that poet number two came in. It was as though they were performing it, rather than just reading it to me. He grabs this gloom by the neck and pulls it up onto a much more positive note:

But tarry not with wretched thought,
For e'en from this can light be brought!

It continues in a brisk fashion, but seems to slow down as it becomes more serious. It then concludes in a manner that is stirring and authoritative, focusing our attention on the Divine itself.

It is an intimate poem in which you feel you are being talked *to*, rather than talked *at*. It is understated in that its form is inferior to its content – when you first hear it, it sounds quite jolly and playful, but as you begin to concentrate on what it is actually saying, you quickly see that it is altogether more profound. It is essentially a message of hope – a message that no one is ever beyond redemption.

Even the worst of us can rise from the pits of depravity into the light of the Divine.

As with all the texts I am publishing in this book, the philosophy here is better described as spiritual rather than religious. There is mention of "God" and "light", concepts compatible with orthodox Christianity, but there is also a healthy dose of mysticism, more reminiscent of Eastern thought than anything we see in Western religion. Perhaps the most obvious example of this is the following four lines:

Until it meets infinity,
A fragment of eternity,
A monumental, beauteous sight
When thought's consumed in purest light.

And the very concept of a "journey with no end" is an endorsement of reincarnation – a journey of life after life after life, as opposed to a journey of one life followed by a static eternity of one extreme or the other.

While many people have been impressed by this poem, works by 16th/17th-century poets aren't everybody's cup of tea. The following poem is very different indeed.

My Guru

High on the hill
Sat the Guru of Tongues,
A sage for all people,
All countries and none.

He dealt me a blow,
He banged me to rights,
He told me my faults,
He put up a fight,
He stifled my reason,
He dared me to laugh,
He throttled my anger;
I cried in my heart.

But then he did something
I'll never forget –
He touched me so gently
My eyes would have wept!
But even that feeling
Was gone with his touch,
My heart was at peace now –
He loved me so much.
His hand on my forehead,
His tender eyes beamed,
He looked at my soul now;
I felt it released.

I travelled away from
This saint on the hill,
But he travelled with me
So silent – so still.
And all was revealed,
As we flew through the air,
To this place and that place

But all of them here,

And all of them now,

And all of them me,

And all of them him,

And all of them you,

And all of them us

All – universal –

Timeless – until

He touched me again,

The saint on the hill.

And so we returned

To the place we first met –

A peak on a mountain

Where he's lived for an age.

Oh how I love you

My guru – my sage!

My Guru has a more popular appeal than *Journey with no End* – its lack of refinement in my opinion more than compensated for by its powerful and direct portrayal of emotion and spiritual feeling.

I received it early one morning while on holiday in Italy in September 2005. Holidays are a good time for me to get messages because I am relaxed.

The sun was rising in the calm untroubled sky. I was sitting by the hotel pool. No one else was there.

While it was coming, I was aware of the poet's accent, which gave me a big clue as to who it was – a well-known 20th-century songwriter. The style and sentiment were quite familiar to me, since I had received messages from him previously. It was delivered very quickly – and although rhythm, rhyming and assonance are used, at no point did I think about them as one would have to if constructing such a poem from scratch.

The guru is the Lama introduced in Chapter 7. I have had to alter the last line of the poem because it reveals his name. While I'm sure there is some link with the Charles Bradlaugh Network, I believe it was the Lama who directed this artist to me, rather than Charles Bradlaugh.

The story told in the poem is, I believe, a factual account of the poet's first meeting with the Lama following his death. It describes, with admirable balance, the two poles of any genuine guru's teaching method: the rough and the smooth, the former being necessary to enable the latter. At first he "banged [him]   to rights", but later "touched [him] so gently/[His] eyes would have wept!". This introduces a description of *shaktipat* – the phenomenon of power being transferred by a guru, often through touch, to induce a mystic state in a disciple. One of the most famous instances of *shaktipat* is brilliantly described by Paramahansa Yogananda in his wonderful book *Autobiography of a Yogi*.

The disciple experiences a state of oneness, which our poet expresses in eight simple lines as follows:

But all of them here,
And all of them now,
And all of them me,
And all of them him,
And all of them you,
And all of them us

All - universal -
Timeless - until

The first six of these lines don't even contain a word more than one syllable long. The description is so straightforward as to be minimalist, and yet none of what he is trying to convey is lost as a result of this word-thrift – on the contrary the simplicity of the language serves to reflect the simplicity of the state itself – a state which is the very essence of simplicity.

The next two poems both reflect the same theme as *My Guru* – that of experiencing greater realisation on the other realms than the communicators ever experienced here. I received them on the same day, in November 2005, while in my sitting-room at home. They didn't come one after another. I got the first one in the morning and the second in the afternoon. In style they are about as different as two poems could possibly be – a reflection of the vast difference in the personalities of their authors.

Sometimes I can get a message by psyching myself up and tuning in – putting out the mental thought of "Here I am if now's a good time for you". Sometimes I might have a particular problem I wish to seek their advice on, or sometimes I might just be making myself available for anything they may wish to give me.

At other times, they tell me they've got something for me. I don't hear anything; it's not "Hey, you down there, listen up". Instead I feel a light, but unmistakable, physical pressure, for example on my hand, shoulder or forehead. This stops when I acknowledge that I have felt it and know what it means. Then it's up to me when and whether to take the message. I might be in the middle of doing something, though I'm sure they would never pick a time when I was doing something important which required all my concentration. Nevertheless, it might not be convenient to stop whatever I was doing and take the message immediately, so I wait for a quiet, appropriate moment to tune in and listen.

On this particular occasion it was convenient to take the message there and then. I started to concentrate and began to feel the vibe of the communicator. Surprisingly I didn't like it at all. It wasn't really bad, as you might feel while doing an exorcism. It just wasn't anything I was used to. It was a bit downbeat and basic, as opposed to being positive and inspirational like the vibe of my guides. I decided not to take the message.

At this point another guide came to me – I'm not sure who – with the kind of vibe I'm familiar with. He told me to stay with it because what was coming was going to be good – despite whatever I might be feeling.

However, even though I went with it, this unfamiliarity proved quite a hindrance. It took me a long time to get it all down – possibly even an hour, a lot longer than a few minutes certainly, even though it's nothing like the quality of *Journey with no End,* for example. The problem was I couldn't get my head round the structure – I didn't know where one line ended and the next began. In fact initially, I wrote the first line as words in a list running down the page.

Freedom on the Beach

Pebble-stoned, shore-lined, foam-sprayed and free,
Fresh breeze, perfect peace, endless sky and me,
Walked down, sun in face, looked out to sea,

Felt good, deep within, a voice said to me -
"Be still, don't fight, love is all - it's free.
Give God holy time - all you need to be -
Yourself - in truth - that's all." We
Will join - as one - all together. He
Told me, there and then, all there is to see;
I know how it is - how I have to be;
I will share it with whoever comes to me.
That's it - all there is - nothing more - just me
And my inner voice - it has set me free.

I was half-way through before I realised that it was a rap song. And it wasn't until later that day that I became aware of the identity of its author, a recently deceased American hip-hop DJ. Possibly he was just picked by a guide because of his skill with words, and his new-found spiritual vision, illustrating the old adage that truth like gold is where you find it.

Just after I had established in my own mind the communicator's identity, the phone rang. It was a good friend of mine – a well-known radio presenter called Mike Allen, with whom I used to do a regular show on LBC (a London radio station) called *The Phenomena Files*. He was the man who introduced hip-hop to the UK in the 1980s, in fact he was recently described by the BBC as a hip-hop legend. Mike doesn't phone me every day – or even every week or every month – so the timing of this call was quite interesting. I told him about the experience and asked him about the rapper I thought it might have been. It turned out that Mike had in fact known the person. He said he was a nice guy, but didn't think he'd be the kind of person who I might get a message from –

which probably he wasn't when he was alive, but as the poem shows, he's changed a lot since then. This may also explain why I hadn't immediately warmed to his vibe.

He describes hearing his inner voice while walking along a beach on another realm. The voice tells him to turn towards spirituality, he agrees and says he will spread the word to whoever comes to him. One interesting feature of it is the feeling of peace which he somehow manages to convey very effectively. My favourite bit is the three lines of what his inner voice actually says to him:

"Be still, don't fight, love is all - it's free.
Give God holy time - all you need to be -
Yourself - in truth - that's all."

"Give God holy time" is a phrase I would never have thought of – but which now I quite like. We should all set time aside for God. Please don't be put off by the word "God" by the way. It's very sad indeed that through the orthodox religious establishment's abuse of power throughout history, so many people have been turned against the very idea of "God" – let alone "religion". On the higher realms there is a better understanding of the true role of religion, enabling people to enjoy the fruits of spirituality without being stifled by the limitation of dogma.

Setting time aside for God could take many forms. The important thing is focus – focus on the Divine Spark which is the essence of all things. It doesn't matter what religion you are – or if you don't have a religion – everyone can find a way of detaching from everyday life and going within. Even if it's only for a few minutes a day – the fruits of these few minutes can help to nourish you throughout your life.

Changed he might be, but he is still the same person. You can take the DJ out of the club, but you can't take the club out of the DJ. The style of the whole "poem" is unashamedly rap-like – as indicated by the staccato rhythm and phrases like "that's all" and "that's it" – but without the expletives, of course! Consider, for example the following three lines:

Yourself - in truth - that's all." We
Will join - as one - all together. He
Told me, there and then, all there is to see;

Mike explained to me that this is sometimes how a rap song performed by two rappers would be done – the first rapper would do a line, onto the end of which the second rapper would add the first word of his following sentence, thereby linking each line together. Interestingly, this DJ usually worked with two rappers, so it was clearly a style he was familiar with.

The next poem is by someone who would almost certainly not be familiar with this style at all. In fact rap hadn't been invented when she was alive, and even if it had, I can't really see it being her scene. She was more into gardening and tea parties than jamming and breakdancing.

The Garden of Infinity

When I look back upon my life,
The times I wept, the times of strife,

When I consider all that passed,

Like worn out clothing fading fast,

Except one thing – one precious fact,

A very special artefact –

The time I spent in love and peace,

That brings a sense of true release,

From foolish thoughts and tired old games,

From rituals with mundane names.

For that is real and that is true,

That will last and then renew

Itself again and yet again;

It grows like flowers in the rain,

Until at last they bloom in time,

At the height of summer's clime,

The love which grows in soil so firm,

The peace which spreads so free of germ.

And all at once the story's told,

A radiant beauty to behold –

One that lingers, one that lasts,

Beyond the grave – the distant past –

Into a rosy future here,

Where all is simple, true and clear!

We know just why we came to be,

We know the journey's meant to be,

And all the answers freely given,

Willingly the questioner's forgiven.

For in this flowery paradise,

The ancient ones give sound advice:

Cultivate your heart, not just your head,

For that will nourish this flowerbed,
This garden of infinity,
Where all is fresh and all is free!
The luminescence shines upon us here,
From skies above, so far, so near,
We bend our knees to weed the ground,
And in the process treasure's found,
Like truth and courage from above,
And most especially peace and love.

She looks at her life from a new perspective – as it is easier to do on the other realms. It's like taking a step back and seeing the whole picture of one's life, in a way that is more detached and philosophical than ever seemed possible while incarnate. Her reminiscence is quite self-critical, but isn't particularly emotional. You almost feel she is saying to herself "What did I think I was doing!? What a silly waste of time!" about much of her life, but she also talks about something which even from a distance is still important to her – something whose value she no doubt now appreciates better than she did in the busy wilderness of this realm. She describes this as "The time I spent in love and peace".

Two phrases which strike me as particularly apt in their portrayal of what no longer matters to her are: "tired old games" and "rituals with mundane names". She is describing the unfulfilling pleasure-seeking and pointless conventions of her time and class, but such criticism could be equally well levied to much of our lives today, whatever our class. Although society today is much less formal than once it was, think of all the boring "rituals" and "tired old games" we still go through. Of course, she is not saying that these things are evil, just that they don't mean as much as we sometimes think they do.

It's heart-warming to see the joy she has found on the realm she now inhabits, free from such limitations. The poem is extremely positive and full of hope for us all – because although she was an accomplished person, we all make mistakes. However, her new-found joy is not a free gift, handed out to everyone like a promotional goodie-bag – she has had to do some thorough soul-searching on her part, which she describes metaphorically as "weeding":

We bend our knees to weed the ground,
And in the process treasure's found,

Much could be read into this couplet. The image of bending knees reminds us of religious devotion, since many orthodox people kneel when they pray, and is symbolic of humility. Weeding is also a dirty job – implying that to find treasure you have to get your hands dirty – it won't be delivered up on a silver platter. The weeds being removed are bad habits and harmful thinking patterns, known in yoga philosophy as negative *samskaras*. It is an interesting analogy, because it suggests that such things grow, as weeds grow, if left unchecked, possibly even to the point of killing the flowers you are actually trying to grow.

As a point of interest, she wasn't fully satisfied with the final result – whether through her fault or mine I don't know. But I certainly consider it worth publishing.

* * *

The final poem I am revealing in this book does not use a rhyming or rhythmic structure as the other poems do, which may be because English was not the original language of the poet. And yet, I regard it as the best poem I've ever channelled:

The Choice

Light billows forth from the highest spheres,
Where reside the gods of old and their acolytes.
In lowest depths, from the very pits,
Blackest black is radiated from the venomous mouths
Of the fallen angels.
But in the midst of light and dark,
Where you and I hold fast to our beliefs,
Where oxen roam, where merchants trade,
And all too often little is accomplished –
Those are the spheres of which I speak today.
For man must die and in his passing make a journey;
His travails are far from over – they have only just begun
Here on the middle planes.
Neither light nor dark, but tinted hues of grey and brown;
Here things continue much as they ever did,
Here they speak insignificant words in garbled form,
Here they dream modest dreams with selfish ends,
Here they rest and play inconsequential games with little
        purpose,
But it troubles them not.
Their only worries are what they cannot get,
Their only feelings are driven by warm emotions,

Not bad, not good - but very, very ordinary.

Oh, would that God could reach this place!

But it is too protected by the armour of small endeavour,

Tiny events, meaningless ambitions -

These are the daily fare on the middle planes.

But, lo, change is upon them, as it is upon us all,

The scythe will reap, the sword will fall!

And into this dull and pointless sphere,

Will come unquestionable certainty and purpose -

For you, for me, for all the inhabitants of that place

For God cannot allow continued waste.

And these are the wasted planes - these middle ones.

So be of good cheer and know

That such empty frivolity cannot last in the Divine Work;

If comedy it be, so shall it have a just end.

And I for one rejoice - albeit from a more lofty seat

Than those who wallow in the middle planes.

Yet often do I attach myself to them, as do you

My eyes have been open to the whole,

Not just the extremes -

The light, the dark, the grey between -

And now I know which of the three is real and which will last.

Throw out the blackest black which belches forth

In a frenzy of violent turbulence,

Lift up the ordinary mundane world of grey and brown,

Which meanders aimlessly

Through backwaters and tributaries - leading nowhere,

And surrender to the Light,

Which lifts and raises you to highest heights.

This is God's plan for us all
Whenever we so choose it!

Driven by deep conviction, the inspired sincerity of this brilliant man virtually leaps off the page. Traditional poetic devices are unnecessary here; the seemingly effortless arrangement of everyday words is quite sufficient to direct the poet's noble passion straight to the reader's heart.

I received this on holiday in Italy in September 2006. It was early in the morning, and we had just got up. When contact started, I asked my wife if she wouldn't mind leaving the room for a few minutes while I took the message, but I was then told clairaudiently, by this very well-mannered, refined gentleman that it was quite alright for "the good lady" to "finish her ablutions". I told her this, but out of respect for the communicating intelligence she decided to leave anyway.

The refined gentleman then proceeded to call on someone he called Brother, who I thought must be a monk, to help him give me the poem. I assumed this must be because he himself was of too high a calibre for me to receive the poem directly from him. It turned out that the Brother was there to help put the poem into vernacular English, making it both easier for me to get, and more accessible to readers. I initially thought it must be a monk because of the word "Brother", but once it was over, I got a clear image of this Brother and realised that he was none other than the author of *My Guru*.

The name of the poet came to me quite quickly, but I didn't believe it, instead dismissing it as wishful thinking on my part. I then got another name which meant nothing to me at all. It sounded Italian, so I asked my wife, who knows much more about Italian culture than I do, if it meant anything to her. It turned out that it was another name of the person whose name I had originally dismissed. This seemed too much to be a coincidence but I still wasn't entirely convinced. I then found out that one of the friends I was on holiday with had bought a picture of this Italian poet the day before without telling any of us and showed it to us there and then. We were not far from this poet's hometown. Stranger still, the exact part of town which he had lived in shared the same name as the villa we were staying in.

This seemed like synchronicity working overtime – but it still wasn't enough for me. It took me some time before I began to feel really confident of his identity – and that confidence came as a result of intuition rather than synchronicity.

In the poem we see an indictment of the mediocrity of "the middle planes". It's not stated exactly which planes are being referred to, but I guess they would include level 2, and probably parts of levels 3 and minus 1 (the least bad lower astral realm) – and would certainly include this realm.

It starts with a brief description of the "highest spheres" and the "lowest depths", before moving on to the main theme: "spheres" which are "in the midst of light and dark".

It is interesting to see the phrase "His (i.e. those on these "spheres") travails are far from over". People often tend to erroneously regard death as a lovely long rest where they have sweet dreams or perfect peace for ever and ever. Clearly this is not the case. "Death" is just a bridge we cross in the great journey of life. And for the average person there are a great deal of "travails" to be done before any degree of noteworthy peace can be achieved.

The poet is not angry or spiteful in any way – there is no trace of negative emotion anywhere in the poem – but he is quite direct in his criticism of what goes on in this land of mediocrity. Consider the following lines:

> Here they speak insignificant words in garbled form,
> Here they dream modest dreams with selfish ends,
> Here they rest and play inconsequential games with little
>   purpose,

Each of these lines starts in quite a mild way – "insignificant words", "modest dreams" and "rest" are nothing to get too worried about – but they each end with a sting in the tale – "garbled form", "selfish ends" and "inconsequential games" all being quite damning in tone. I think the purpose of this could be to subtly illustrate that mediocrity seems fine *at first*, but is in fact not as harmless as it looks, in that it holds people back from experiencing the joy of spiritual freedom. He goes on in the same vein:

> But it troubles them not.
> Their only worries are what they cannot get,
> Their only feelings are driven by warm emotions,
> Not bad, not good - but very, very ordinary.

He is clearly far from ambivalent about what people do on the middle planes, but he is also very restrained – careful never to polemicise too vehemently, a bit like a compassionate schoolteacher watching children mucking about when they should be doing their homework. Likewise, notice that he says earlier "tinted hues of grey and brown" instead of just "grey", conceding that there is an element of colour, albeit not a very vivid one.

Worrying about "what [we] cannot get" is something that most people would agree was "very, very ordinary", but feelings "driven by warm emotions" would be regarded as "good" by many people. What he is reminding us here is that there is more to human feeling than just the basic sentimentality we all at times indulge in.

I like the next two lines very much:

Oh, would that God could reach this place!
But it is too protected by the armour of small endeavour,

The first line is something which I would never think of saying, but I can see what he means. The reason I wouldn't say it is because God is in all places at all times – God is the essence of everything, so to imply that God cannot reach a particular place is absurd. However, this isn't what he is driving at. He means "would that people would allow the Divine to manifest in its true greatness throughout their lives", or perhaps even "would that God would burst forth and transmute all this ordinariness into something greater". But that can't happen while "the armour of small endeavour", i.e. the mindset of mediocrity, prevents it.

Nevertheless, there will come a time when this will not be so:

For God cannot allow continued waste.
And these are the wasted planes - these middle ones.
So be of good cheer and know
That such empty frivolity cannot last in the Divine Work;
If comedy it be, so shall it have a just end.

There will come a time when the children of mediocrity will stop their foolish games and go back to their lessons. This might strike some people as depressing at first, but instead of being depressed we are told that we should "be of good cheer". Likewise "comedy" here doesn't of course mean "comedy" in the sense that it's used these days, it means having "a just end" – a very positive, spiritually empowering concept.

* * *

The number of people who think they are going to heaven is much greater than the number who think they are going to hell. But the people who think they're heading for heaven may be amazed to discover what the afterlife is really like – according to this poet quite ordinary for many people. What does it really take to get to the higher realms? What would someone on level 5 say "being good" meant? A lot more than leading an ordinary life – that's for sure.

I felt inspired to call this poem *The Choice* because, as is explained at the very end, we all have to make our own individual choice about when we are going to start taking the opportunity to experience something more than the "wasted planes" have to offer. The poet's call for us to "surrender to the Light" is a heartfelt plea – not that we should submit to some man-made system of morality, but that we should be lifted and raised "to highest heights". This makes the poem much more than just an indictment of mediocrity – it makes it a shining message of spiritual hope.

CHAPTER 10

Ascended Masters

"From death lead me to immortality"
Brihadaranyaka Upanishad

"You will not kill me, for I am not destined to die," he announced fearlessly.

This stirringly defiant quotation from Homer's *Iliad* (XXII.13), not only demonstrated a degree of erudition, but also, accompanied with the action which immediately followed, proved beyond doubt to the thousands of onlookers his phenomenal power, for, no sooner had he finished speaking, than he quite literally vanished into thin air – thereby escaping the wicked emperor Domitian.

Apollonius of Tyana had come up against Roman authorities before. He'd got himself in trouble for treasonable talk against Nero, the crazy singing emperor who infamously fiddled while Rome burnt – or so it is believed. What Apollonius had actually said was little more than common sense, but under the rule of a tyrant there is surely no crime greater than common sense – particularly when directed against the tyrant himself.

Tigellinus, the emperor's depraved advisor, had him arrested. But when he came to read the scroll on which the charge against Apollonius had been written, he discovered that it was blank. Doubtless shocked, but nevertheless determined, Tigellinus took him to his own secret court and interrogated him in private.

Fortunately, what would fill most men with a sickening sense of dread, was apparently little more than a bit of fun for Apollonius. Eventually, overawed by his captive's relaxed defiance, including the outrageous statement that Nero would show more dignity by silence than by singing, Tigellinus, mad though he may well have been, proved capable enough of reason to realise that he had no power over Apollonius, concluding that he had no choice but to release him.

Who Apollonius of Tyana really was, or what he was like, no one knows for certain. According to Philostratus' *Life of Apollonius*, he was affable, witty, handsome, highly principled, fearless and endowed with remarkable supernormal abilities. I have no idea how accurately history has recorded his life and his extraordinary adventures, but if the above stories are in fact true, together with the testimony to his fine character, I would venture to guess that he was no less than an Adept, and quite possibly a Master, an Ascended Master or perhaps even more than that.

But true or not, I do not doubt that such things are possible. And not just in the questionable depths of ill-documented antiquity – but at any time, even today. Mastery is no more a gift than being psychic is a gift – in fact less so, in that Mastery is incomparably above just being psychic, and therefore requires vastly more effort. But the very fact that it requires effort means that if sufficient effort is exerted, it is eventually achievable – however distant such a goal may seem to most of us.

* * *

In order to understand the ancient concept of Mastery, it is necessary to understand yoga philosophy. Sadly, the word "yoga" is often misunderstood today. People mistake it for just another fashionable way of staying healthy and fit. While it is true that a branch of yoga called *Hatha* Yoga was indeed designed for this purpose, its ultimate goal was originally very different to what I would imagine to be the goal in the minds of many Hatha Yoga practitioners in the modern West – which is often just to look good.

The original goal of Hatha Yoga was to prepare the body for the inner beauty of real yoga – "yoga" meaning "union", implying "union with the Divine" – which could be achieved by the practice of various yogas such as Raja Yoga, the form of yoga ascribed to the sage Patanjali, associated with mental and psychic control; Bhakti Yoga – the yoga of devotion; Karma Yoga – the yoga of service (see Chapter 12); Mantra Yoga – the yoga of sacred sound; and Kundalini Yoga – an advanced form of yoga which focuses directly on the mystical power located at the base of the spine, known as *Kundalini*, or "the serpent power".

Without the power of Kundalini we could not live. And even if we could, there would be no point, since mastering the control and use of this power – according to yoga philosophy – is our one and only reason for being alive.

The vast majority of us use only a fraction of the full potential of Kundalini. Those great spiritual aspirants who have, through lifetimes of dedicated work in service to others and rigorous self-development, learned to raise this mighty power up the spine into the higher chakras (or "psychic centres"), are termed Adepts or Masters – the term "Master" usually referring to someone of a higher degree of attainment than the term "Adept". Such people are far above the psychic stage – they have developed psychic abilities, and then, retaining only the abilities which they use in service to others, taken their powers onto a higher level – a level of profound intuitive awareness. Notice, however, that although they are above the psychic stage, they have nevertheless had to go through it. You cannot reach the highest states of consciousness without doing so. People who talk glibly of spiritual "Enlightenment", without ever mentioning the need to develop and then transmute psychic powers, show that they don't really know what Enlightenment is, and that they don't appreciate just how great a meditative experience it is possible to have.

This type of experience is not exclusive to the cave-dwelling Himalayan yogis of old. It is perfectly possible for someone who has never even heard the term "Kundalini" to enter an advanced higher state of consciousness. As long ago as 1798, the great poet William Wordsworth, who at that time would not have had access in the West to the yoga teachings which are available to us today, describes a state which strikes me as remarkably similar to a state of meditation brought on by a Kundalini rise. Notice especially how he describes a state comparable to physical death, and mentions "an eye".

Of aspect more sublime; that blessed mood,
In which the burthen of the mystery,
In which the heavy and the weary weight
Of all this unintelligible world,
Is lightened: – that serene and blessed mood,
In which the affections gently lead us on, –
Until, the breath of this corporeal frame
And even the motion of our human blood
Almost suspended, we are laid asleep

In body, and become a living soul:
While with an eye made quiet by the power
Of harmony, and the deep power of joy,
We see into the life of all things.

Extracted from: LINES – COMPOSED A FEW MILES ABOVE TINTERN ABBEY, ON REVISITING THE BANKS OF THE WYE DURING A TOUR. JULY 13, 1798

In his commentary on a series of teachings called *The Nine Freedoms* for which he acted as the channel, Dr King talks in fascinating, and to the best of my knowledge, unprecedented, detail about the experiences caused by the raising of the Kundalini, including the fact that when the Kundalini is raised to the Christ Centre, or "third eye", the aspirant's body virtually ceases to function: their blood flow having almost stopped, their breathing having become almost imperceptible.

In order to avoid any possible confusion in readers' minds, I would like to take this opportunity to state quite definitely that, although I have experienced certain basic mystic states in which I have felt tremendously at peace, I am a very long way from being the calibre of an Adept or a Master.

Nevertheless it is important to remember that even Adepts and Masters, however great they may be, still have more to learn. They will continue to be subject to reincarnation until they are able, at will, to raise the Kundalini to their highest chakra, the crown chakra, thereby inducing the deepest mystic state of all: Cosmic Consciousness – the most complete realisation of the oneness of all things that it is possible for any mortal to experience.

Every life lesson we ever learn – whether we realise it or not – is leading us, albeit in most cases very slowly, to this pinnacle of evolution. After this there is no need to continue to reincarnate upon Earth because every lesson we ever needed to learn has been learned.

The aspirant has now completely mastered terrestrial experience.

But this is not the end.

It is the beginning of a greater life – of a totally spiritual existence.

The Master has a choice of leaving the Earth, or remaining here and going through what is known as the Initiation of Ascension, which makes him or her immortal. This means that they will have a body which will never age. They will not be victim to the ravages of time, they will never become old in the way that we do – a concept which we find in ancient Eastern thought. They no longer require this experience. Instead of illness and senility, age will bring them wisdom and spiritual opportunity. That's not to say they will have the same body for all eternity; they may – in full consciousness – decide for some very definite reason to change their body, but when they do so, they will have control over the change.

Freedom from childhood and old age, not to mention all the multifarious other limitations we mortals must undergo, makes Ascension seem very appealing – a magnificent reward for lives of spiritual effort. But please don't run away with the idea that Ascended Masters just lounge around, resting on their laurels, enjoying the fruits of their labours. On the contrary, they work harder than ever.

Their choice to remain here, as opposed to leaving the Earth completely, is a great sacrifice, made with the mass of humanity in mind. They do not need to remain on Earth for their own sakes, they choose to in order to help us, which they do in many different ways, mostly behind the scenes, totally unknown to the very people they are working to help, and thus demonstrating a level of altruism which shows just how advanced they really are. For more information about one particular fascinating aspect of their work, I would strongly recommend a book called *Operation Earth Light – a glimpse into the world of the Ascended Masters* by Brian C. Keneipp.

Together they form an "organisation", for want of a better term, called "The Spiritual Hierarchy of Earth", also known as "The Great White Brotherhood" – though the latter is perhaps a somewhat misleading name in that it causes some people to infer that its Members are all male or all white, which is certainly not the case. Many are female and in fact Dr King has stated that white-skinned Members are actually in the minority. "White" refers to "white magic" as opposed to "black magic" – it has nothing whatever to do with skin colour.

The Spiritual Hierarchy is also supplemented by certain individuals who are not ascended, but have very useful special skills. At its head is The Lord Babaji, whose level of evolution is above that of even an Ascended Master (see Chapter 12).

Although they may seem remote to our everyday lives, it is important to remember that their presence on Earth is vital not just to our spiritual evolution, but to our very survival. Dr King went as far as to say that if the Hierarchy were to leave Earth we wouldn't last more than about three and a half days without them.

Instances of The Lord Babaji or any of the Ascended Masters revealing themselves are few and far between – despite the many claims…

* * *

There are, in my opinion, four explanations for false mediumistic communications with Ascended Masters. (1) The medium is deliberately faking; (2) The medium is deluded by their own fanciful imagination or by a mental illness; (3) The entity is deliberately deceiving the medium by pretending to be more advanced than they are in order to cause confusion; (4) The medium has mistaken a comparatively ordinary entity for a much more advanced one.

Possibilities (1) and (2) speak for themselves, but (3) and (4), I feel, require some elucidation.

With regard to possibility (3) – there are entities in the lower astral realms who deliberately contact channellers and pretend to be more advanced than they are. This could perhaps simply be because they are perverse enough to find it amusing, or because their sick egos find it pleasurable to be falsely revered as spiritual Masters. But, more sinister than this, it is also possible that they may deliberately wish to cause confusion among spiritual seekers, thereby preventing good people from finding and benefiting from true wisdom.

This deception results in a plethora of false teachings – from the banal and ridiculous to the sophisticatedly deceptive. The former, common sense can tell you doesn't come from an advanced Master, whereas the latter has the most potential for harm. A communicator who talks of "love" and "peace" in pleasant, flowery language, who fills his "teaching" with true spirituality meanwhile lacing it with falsehood, could be very hard to discern from a communicator with a genuine, completely spiritual message.

That's why it's so important to learn how to discriminate between the true and the false, through analysing the messages. Be sceptical. Ask yourself what the message is really saying – very often the answer will be: not a lot. Ask yourself if the message is really a guide to building a better world, or just a tacit endorsement of ordinary life. Ask yourself if it's telling you what you *need* to hear, or just what you *want* to hear.

But most important of all, of course, always apply your intuition. And the more sincere and truly determined you are in your quest for truth, the more effective will be your intuition when assessing a teaching for its truth content.

Unlike possibility (3), possibility (4) is not the result of any deliberate wrongdoing, and, consequently, in my opinion, is less dangerous. A channeller might be getting a message from a relatively ordinary guide who is giving genuinely good teaching, support or advice, but may mistake him or her for a great Master. This comes about as a result of the channeller's lack of experience.

This kind of thing can happen to non-mediums as well. Someone might have a guide or guardian angel who they are vaguely aware of, and mistakenly believe that they are some great being. I was fascinated once when I was in America to meet an ordinary Christian who thought that Jesus (who I believe to be above the level of an Ascended Master) had given him some petty personal advice which was quite specific and had in fact turned out to be correct. Now the idea that a great being like Jesus would be advising Joe Bloggs in this way is not credible – but, it is possible that this man was in fact listening to his guardian angel.

You might wonder why guardian angels and guides don't tell their channellers or protégés that they've made a mistake, and give them their real identity. Well, they might try, but they might just not be able to get the person to receive and understand such a message – particularly if the person is already absolutely positive that they know who it is. This false certainty is often the result of, or at least exacerbated by, ego – it sounds much more glamorous, for example, to say you're in touch with an Ascended Master than with an unknown discarnate schoolteacher called Jack Smith. In the case of the American Christian, such a person would probably not even have believed in guardian angels or guides – so as far as he would have been concerned there were only two main possibilities: Jesus or the devil – and, unsurprisingly, he had picked Jesus.

Given that the guardian angel or guide may not be able to correct the channeller or protégé, you may wonder why they don't just cease the communication altogether. This is where I really feel sorry for the communicator – what a choice to have to make! "Do I help this person or group, allowing them to believe that I am someone much more advanced than I really am, or do I just leave them without any guidance?" No doubt there are all kinds of considerations to be taken into account when weighing up the pros and cons of continuing versus discontinuing communication or guidance.

An understanding of one simple principle could sort out a huge proportion of all the various types of cases of false claims relating to contact with extremely elevated intelligences – in the minds both of the medium or protégé and of those seeking to evaluate such claims. That is the "sieve principle" which you may recall from Chapter 4. It is only possible for direct communication to take place between someone on this realm and an advanced person on another, if the person here is of a degree of advancement comparable to that of the communicator. So an ordinary medium, who leads a fairly ordinary life, and does not have a genuinely unusual degree of spiritual (as opposed to psychic) perception, certainly couldn't contact an Ascended Master – nor, I'm afraid, could an ordinary Christian get a specific message about some personal triviality direct from Jesus.

While we're on the subject, I should state for the record that while my guides may be more advanced than the average discarnate – they are certainly not Adepts, Masters or Ascended Masters. I am quite simply not advanced enough to channel intelligences of such a high calibre. Notice also that while the poems and texts which I have channelled (see Chapters 1, 8 and 9) are spiritual, they are not spiritual *teachings*, and are on a lower level than the communications received by the mediums discussed later in this chapter.

* * *

Moving on to the positive, I shall now go into accounts of people who I believe genuinely have had contact with Ascended Masters.

The *Autobiography of a Yogi*, by Paramahansa Yogananda, founder of the Self-Realisation Fellowship, is packed with dazzling tales of illuminated Masters and the miracles they perform. He even tells the story of his own Master, Sri Yukteswar, visiting him in a Bombay hotel room three months after his passing. Yogananda, roused from his spiritual practice by a great light, was overwhelmed with joy to see his beloved guru. He hugged him tightly; he was in a physical body, identical to that which he had inhabited while incarnate. They spent two hours together, during which time Sri Yukteswar used both speech and telepathy to communicate.

Particularly unusual are the stories Yogananda tells relating to the mighty Lord Babaji. Unimaginably elevated in every sense – The Lord Babaji's wisdom, love, and brilliance defy our feeble powers of comprehension – and the true nature of his work is no doubt equally unfathomable. But one of his roles which is relatively straightforward for us to grasp is that of *guru*, or teacher. It is this role which Yogananda focuses on.

He does not teach openly. He does not run advertised workshops in public places. He does not have an ashram with an address and a billboard outside. So anyone calling themselves "Babaji" who does teach openly is either a fake – or, more likely, just a different Babaji, which is quite possible since "Babaji" simply means "revered father".

The great Master Lahiri Mahasaya, who was the Master of Sri Yukteswar, first met The Lord Babaji when he was 32. He was working as an accountant at the time, in Danapur, when he was told that he was to be transferred to Ranikhet in the Himalayas, 500 miles away. Having heard that the mountains of the region were home to holy sages, he decided to explore the area in the hope of seeing one.

To his great surprise he heard someone call his name, and a little while later came face to face with a yogi who greeted him warmly. With a single touch to Lahiri's forehead, the mysterious guru unlocked the buried memories of his student's former life: with tears of joy, Lahiri now recognised The Lord Babaji as his Master.

He was told to drink some oil, which presumably had some special quality, and then to go to the river and lie down, which he did for some time – taking the opportunity to muse over what had happened. He was then met by another of The Lord Babaji's students, who led him to a magnificent palace, which, though physical to the touch, had been miraculously created by the phenomenal power of the Master's visualisation, in order to quench a latent materialistic desire which Lahiri had felt long, long ago, thereby releasing him from this particular karmic shackle. It also served as the venue for an initiation by his Master into a type of yoga called "Kriya Yoga".

The following morning, having thoroughly admired his exquisite surroundings, The Lord Babaji told Lahiri to close his eyes, which he of course obeyed. When he opened them again, the palace had disappeared.

After a period of several days, just before Lahiri left his guru to descend into the worldly clatter below, in order to be of service to his less advanced brothers and sisters as a teacher and living example of the glories of spiritual life, The Lord Babaji made the generous promise of saying he would appear before his student whenever he called him.

A few days later Lahiri found himself spending time with people who found it hard to believe the amazing story of his time in the mountains. Remembering his guru's promise, he summoned him into his presence. The Lord Babaji did indeed appear, and his appearance had the desired dramatic affect on the disbelievers.

But what a mistake!

The holy Master reprimanded his disciple for abusing his privilege. After all, a Master, particularly one of The Lord Babaji's lofty station, should only be summoned in exceptional circumstances. As a result this remarkable, Divinely bestowed privilege was retracted.

It is worth noting that Masters are not always what people expect them to be. Although a Master is never selfish or cruel, he or she may at times appear so, particularly to someone unversed in the rigours of the spiritual path.

It is said that The Lord Babaji once picked up a log from the fire and burned a disciple's shoulder with it, after which he put his hand on the shoulder and healed the wound. An apparently bizarre thing to do, but his motive had in fact been to burn up some of the disciple's karma, which otherwise would have caused him to burn to death.

Similarly, there is a tale of a man coming before The Lord Babaji pleading to be allowed to follow him as a disciple. The Master did not respond. The man continued, saying that if he couldn't be accepted as a disciple, then he would jump off a cliff. With apparent callousness, The Lord Babaji told him to go ahead and jump – which he did. Afterwards, however, the great Master revived the man's battered corpse and told him that having passed this test he was now ready to be his disciple.

The mysterious work of the Masters is not confined to the East. There is a mysterious gentleman, usually known as "Count St Germain", about whom many strange tales have been told regarding his appearances throughout the past few centuries of Western history. Dr King recounted a story he had come across that on one occasion the Count had told someone that he was going to England in order to inspire a man named George Stephenson – the engineer to whom the invention of the railway locomotive is attributed.

The Theosophist Madame Blavatsky (about whom – more later), quotes an article which talks in some detail about his unusual life. According to this article he was said to be hundreds of years old (which as an Ascended Master of course he could have been). He was able to tell stories about events of the distant past with the clarity one would associate with an eye-witness account. He mingled among Europe's elite – particularly, it seems, in France – causing a great stir. He attended dinner parties, but refused to eat anything; he would only eat specially-prepared oatmeal, groats or white chicken meat, and, occasionally, drink a little wine. A brilliant conversationalist, and fluent in many languages, he would speak with confidence and authority, displaying a prodigious knowledge of a host of subjects.

The article describes him as an alchemist. He talked of the fusion of several diamonds into one huge stone, and also supposedly demonstrated the transmutation of metal into the purest gold. His activities varied from the seemingly frivolous, such as giving mysterious cosmetics to wealthy ladies (to which, if true at all, there no doubt lay a higher purpose than was immediately apparent), to facilitating the accession of Catherine II to the Russian throne. Reportedly possessing an array of different identities, he is associated with various names, perhaps most notably that of "Rakoczy", some believing that he was the son of a Prince Rakoczy of Transylvania. The Theosophist Charles Leadbeater claimed that the Count was, among others, Christian Rosenkreuz, the legendary founder of Rosicrucianism.

Having now mentioned Theosophy, it would seem fitting to go into more detail about this fascinating school of esoteric knowledge.

Helena Petrovna Blavatsky (1831-1891) was undoubtedly a remarkable woman and I am a huge fan of hers. The fact that, even today, there are people who feel the need to besmirch her reputation, only serves, to my mind at least, as a testament to her greatness. That's not to say that she never made a mistake, or that I agree with everything she ever said, wrote or did, but, if respect for another were dependent on faultlessness or total accord, no one would ever respect anyone.

She was a vivacious, witty, sociable young woman – though her attitude to life changed somewhat in her mid teens when she began to develop a serious interest in mysticism – an interest nurtured by a freemason called Prince Alexander Golitsyn, who was the son of a family friend. However, despite her metaphysical inclinations, which had been evident since childhood, she was of an inherently volatile disposition – a trait which manifested throughout her life.

She was married to a much older man, Nikifor Blavatsky, at the tender age of 17. She refused her elderly husband the conjugal rights he demanded, and after a relatively short period of time together she ran away to begin a new life which turned out to be packed with adventures unthinkable for a young lady from an aristocratic Russian family.

Most important among her many extraordinary experiences, was her contact with the great Masters, also known as Mahatmas, including The Master Morya, whom she had seen in visions since childhood – and finally met face to face, as it were, in London on her twentieth birthday; and The Master Koot Hoomi (also spelled "Kuthumi"), thought by Leadbeater to be the same intelligence as Pythagoras, whom she met for the first time in 1868. She believed that these Masters had lived in the same bodies for hundreds of years.

In New York City in 1875, together with others, including her great supporter Colonel Henry Steel Olcott, she founded The Theosophical Society, which was to be used as a vehicle for the wisdom of the Great Ones.

According to reports her mode of authorship was unusual to say the least. She would be writing away vigorously when she would stop, with a degree of suddenness, and raise her head, as though looking at something invisible, close in front of her, and then carry on, apparently hastily copying down what she had seen. Many of the quotations she cites, we are told, could not have been found in the books available to her at the time. A gentleman named Prof Carson, with whom she stayed for a time while she was writing *Isis Unveiled* commented that if she had indeed memorised all the quotations she used prior to writing, then she was demonstrating a feat of memorisation even more remarkable than her professed faculty of psychic vision.

Colonel Olcott, who would work with her until late into the night, assisting her where necessary in her herculean marathon of writing, recounted an interesting incident which began with his questioning whether or not she had got a particular quotation right. She was sure she had, but nevertheless, in an altered state of consciousness, directed him to a corner of the room, in which he found the two volumes required. He stated that he had not been aware of their presence in the building until that moment, and that after he had put them back, he glanced back at the corner to find that they had both inexplicably vanished.

Her personality would appear to undergo dramatic changes while she was working – in fact she would virtually become different people, with different handwriting, opinions, knowledge of English, and mood. She said that the degree of consciousness retained when her body was taken over in this way by one of the great sages would vary; sometimes she would be fully aware of everything that was going on, sometimes not.

In the "Proem" in her monumental and highly complex work *The*

Secret Doctrine, she describes, albeit in tantalising brevity, seeing "an archaic manuscript", before her "eye", which is no doubt referring to her "third eye". One could speculate that this was a form of remote viewing.

Although much of her writing is frankly somewhat impenetrable, we should be careful not to underestimate her legacy. She promoted spiritual concepts which had never been promulgated in that way before, and which have had a lasting effect on the New Age movement.

It is believed that Alice Bailey (1880-1949), who was at one time a member of the Theosophical Society, wrote in collaboration with a great sage called Djwhal Khul (also spelled "Djwal Kul"), often simply known as "The Tibetan". According to the appendix of her autobiography, her – or *his* – classic work entitled *A Treatise on Cosmic Fire* was composed in four distinctly different ways: (1) Clairaudiently – the Tibetan would dictate; (2) Telepathically – usually allowing Alice Bailey to use her own words, though occasionally he would use his own knowledge of English, which required minor editing; (3) Clairvoyantly – she would see a symbol which she could then describe, or an ancient text, written in ideographs or symbols, which she was able to translate by virtue of an enhanced sense of awareness. Any mistakes in her translation would then be corrected by the Tibetan. (4) By leaving the body while asleep at night – certain parts of the work are the result of what she either saw or heard while out of the body.

Interestingly, according to her writings, although she worked for The Tibetan, her own Master was The Master Koot Hoomi, who had first contacted her when she just 15, at a time when she was depressed and volatile. She had been sitting alone in the drawing-room one Sunday morning, when the Master had walked in, wearing beautifully tailored European clothes and a turban. He talked to her briefly about the great work ahead of her, and told her to improve her behaviour – which indeed she did, so successfully in fact, that her family got quite worried, wondering what had happened to the old Alice they had known.

She tells us that her contact with The Tibetan didn't start until she was 39. She was outside, on a hill near her home, sitting down, thinking, when suddenly she heard what sounded like a musical note. She then heard a voice asking if she was willing to cooperate in the writing of certain books. Her reply was firmly in the negative. He tried to persuade her, but she was adamant that she wanted no part in it. Three weeks later she was asked again – and her answer was the same – but finally she was persuaded to at least give it a go – won over by curiosity, more than anything else. This was to herald the beginning of her work on *Initiation, Human and Solar*.

It is thought that Theosophist Mabel Collins (1851-1927) was in touch with an intelligence called The Master Hilarion – and that it was from him she received the wonderful little book *Light on the Path*, by clairaudient dictation, in the 1880s. It is also believed that she received another work from him – though curiously the link between her and The Master Hilarion mysteriously seemed to dissolve when it was only half completed. As a result she decided to finish it herself, but later she reportedly regained her rapport with Hilarion, and he gave her the rest of the text as it should have been.

* * *

I am not, I'm afraid, advanced enough to be able to do much more than guess at the evolutionary status of some of the "Masters" mentioned in this chapter. I do not know, for example, if The Master Hilarion is in The Spiritual Hierarchy or not – nor do I know whether or not he is Ascended, or even a Master at all – he may "only" (for want of a better word) be an Adept or some kind of Initiate on the higher realms. Nor can I vouch with complete certainty for the unwavering veracity of many of the claims I have recounted here. I do, however, believe firmly in the deep sincerity of towering figures such as Paramahansa Yogananda, Madame Blavatsky, Annie Besant, Alice Bailey, and Mabel Collins – their high spiritual calibre evidenced by the quality of their work.

Members of the Hierarchy with whom Dr King has had contact include The Lord Babaji, The Lord Maitreya, who is one of the most elevated of all the Ascended Masters, Count St Germain, and The Master Saint Goo-Ling, with whom, to the best of my knowledge no one other than Dr King has ever claimed contact. He is one of its most prominent Members, about whom little is known other than that he is the Hierarchy's "Keeper of the Seal"; is an expert on the Law of Karma; has been in the same body for over 2000 years; and speaks with a marked East Asian accent. It has been suggested to me since Dr King's passing that the name "Goo-Ling" could possibly be the Chinese words *gǔ líng* – meaning "ancient spirit".

Dr King has also stated that the great Indian yogi, Swami Vivekananda (1863-1902), is now in The Great White Brotherhood. Swami Vivekananda is one of my all-time heroes, a great yogi who combined deep spirituality with a commanding intellect. A leading disciple of the holy saint, Sri Ramakrishna, he brought Eastern wisdom to the West, when he represented Hinduism at The World's Parliament of Religions held in Chicago in 1893, in a speech as remarkable for its brilliant oratory as its profound wisdom. He was said to be given help sometimes in preparing his lectures by voices he heard at night, often while he was in bed – suggesting a type of advanced clairaudience. He continued to spread the Vedanta philosophy in America, Britain and other parts of Europe, later returning to his native India. He died at the age of 39 years 5 months and 24 days, thus fulfilling his own prophesy that he would die before the age of 40.

One evening over dinner with Dr King – just the two of us – I mentioned to him that there had recently been a book published that was highly critical of Madame Blavatsky. His reaction surprised me – he stood up, walked around the room and said emphatically that whatever anyone might say about her, she was in The Great White Brotherhood now. I did not take this to mean that she has necessarily ascended, but that she is in some way involved directly in the work of the Ascended Masters.

The Hierarchy has used Retreats in various locations around the world, including Grand Teton, Mount Shasta and Castle Peak in the USA; Luxor in Egypt; Mount Kilimanjaro in Tanzania; Ben MacDhui in Scotland; the Andes; Sri Lanka; and, of course, the Himalayas. On one occasion while in Scotland Dr King projected from his physical body and met a female Ascended Master. He described her as being about 5'2" or 5'3", dressed in a long hooded robe, and appearing to be middle-aged – though she was in fact hundreds of years older than that. On another occasion, also in a state of projection, Dr King witnessed the actual Initiation ceremony of the Ascension of a young girl of about eighteen.

My personal experience of The Spiritual Hierarchy is, as far as I am concerned, a testament, and shining tribute, to Dr King's degree of advancement rather than my own. It was only possible as a result of a particular Initiation Dr King had given me, and, of course, because of Dr King's ability to communicate directly with its Members.

It was necessary for a Member of The Spiritual Hierarchy to be positioned in a special, metaphysically significant location while a certain operation was underway. Hard though it is even for me to believe, I was asked by Dr King if I could go to such a location, the nearest of which was in Scotland, and stay there for a few days during which I would actually be a Member of the Hierarchy – *for that time only*. Of course, I was thrilled to be given such an amazing opportunity – if somewhat apprehensive at its magnitude.

I didn't have to *do* anything at all – I just had to be in the right place at the right time. A simple task, most definitely, but the awareness of its great importance kept me on my toes, as it were. I ate, slept, did some writing, and the time seemed to pass uneventfully. I didn't have any dramatic psychic experience, and, naturally, I didn't have any contacts with Ascended Masters. But I did have a change of perception – I understood, more than ever before, my own superficiality in comparison with the great depth of a true Master. I began to dimly appreciate the profundity of their capacity for realisation – that if I were to realise something, which an Ascended Master had realised – although the subject of the realisation might be the same, the extent of it would be very different indeed.

I was privileged to take part in two more "Great White Brotherhood Standbys", as they were called. Such an experience could never be repeated now that Dr King has passed on, and will always be among the most cherished experiences of my life.

CHAPTER 11

Religion

"All men have need of the gods"
Homer

Religion is the way people traditionally express their relationship with the Divine – whatever they might conceive "the Divine" to be. When seeking to understand someone's faith, one of the first questions to ask a believer might be whether they believe in just one God, in Gods plural, or in some other concept of the Divine. Perhaps the next question might be how the message of the religion had reached humanity from its source.

It is not my intention in this chapter to try to give an exhaustive account of all cases of claimed contacts with God, Gods, Divine emissaries or other beings associated with religion – or to explain the ideologies which have resulted from such contacts. Nor do I wish to pass judgement over the authenticity of any of the beliefs recounted here. I simply want to illustrate how important this kind of contact – in all its various forms and interpretations – is to cultures all over the globe. Even though religion now plays a much less dominant role in many societies than it once did, it would be wrong to deny the debt the modern world owes to the religious values which have contributed to the foundation of what we now call civilisation.

Devas

But before getting too involved in the field of religious contact, I would like to talk about a kind of "god" which has very little to do with religion – or at least with religion in the way most people tend to think of it in the West.

There are countless numbers of these gods, existing all around us, all the time, for the most part unseen, and unknown to the vast majority of humankind. Even though I am clairvoyant, I have never seen one – but I have felt their presence, particularly in the countryside, and I have no doubt that they exist.

I would call them "devas", but they have many names – "nature spirits" and "fairies" perhaps being the most common.

It is unfortunate that belief in fairies has become synonymous with delusion and impracticality. It is strange that it is relatively acceptable to believe in angels, ghosts, guides, extraterrestrials and a variety of religious belief systems which are considerably at odds with scientific materialism, whereas if you tell someone you believe in fairies, or, more outrageous still, have seen one, you are likely to be met with an expression of embarrassment or confusion at best – and at worst outright ridicule.

This is a great shame. It constitutes yet another example of how much we – humanity as a whole – have divorced ourselves both from nature and from spiritual experience.

Devas are responsible for looking after nature. They are associated with plants, rivers, mountains, weather etc. We rely on them all the time, for the most part without even knowing it. Every time we light a fire, for example, we are invoking a deva. Without the devas no fire would light. Some might respond to that by saying that fire either lights or doesn't depending on various physical, scientifically understood variables. This is of course true, but it's the devas who are responsible for making these variables work to produce the expected result.

As well as working with physical things, they are also very susceptible to our thoughts. If we are filled with feelings like hatred, resentment, bitterness, selfishness or violent emotion, we are, whether we realise it or not, affecting our environment for the worse. It is a kind of pollution – of a very serious nature. Consider all the negativity emitted into the ethers by most of the cities in the world – particularly those ravaged by crime or war, and other "freer" places engaged in excessive pleasure-seeking and hedonism. The unspiritual energy which is emanated goes to the devas who then use it according to the Law of Karma. They have no choice but to create violent weather conditions, resulting in floods, droughts and other forms of devastation, because these things, according to Karma, are the natural result of the energy we give them. It's not that the devas enjoy watching us suffer, it's that they, unlike us, have chosen to work exactly according to the Law of Karma – which demands this kind of result.

On the positive side they also, of course, respond to the good energy we send out. You can try this for yourself next time you go for a walk in the countryside. Try to feel a real love for nature, a real appreciation for the beauty around you. Try to become aware of the fact that life is all around you, expressing itself in countless different ways. Think about the debt we owe the devas for all their work in helping us to gain the experience that Karma requires of us. Thank them for their work. Tune in. Allow yourself to be aware of their presence. This can be a really beautiful experience. Any love you send them, they will respond to. This will teach you much more about devas than anything I could write here.

You may not see one. Few people do. And you shouldn't expect to either – this kind of exercise should not be motivated by the desire to have an amazing paranormal experience. It's a gentle, harmonious practice, which will only work if you treat it as such.

Having said that, it could well be that devas are in fact seen much more than is supposed – but that people are unwilling to report their experience for fear of what other people might say. One of the few people I've come across willing to talk about having seen devas is my wife, Alyson, who reports one incident as follows:

"I was alone in my mother's house. It was a sunny, but chilly, afternoon and I was planning to do some gardening. I went to get an old gardening coat from the cupboard.

"To my utter astonishment, sitting on the tightly-packed coat-rack, was a strange little humanoid creature, no more than a few inches tall. It stood up when it saw me, and for a second or two we stared at each other in mutual amazement at the other's presence; it seemed almost as shocked to have been disturbed as I was to find it there.

"It was a little elf. It seemed physical, but not completely so… it had a wispy quality about it, indistinct, almost like a water-colour in 3D, as though made of a kind of matter which was somehow finer than the world we perceive around us on a day-to-day basis. It was wearing a tall, pointed, rimless brown hat – in fact everything about it was brown… various shades of light brown, a little like a cappuccino which has been gently stirred a couple of times.

"It raised its arms, in a diving pose, jumped up, and plunged headfirst into the coats. I was very sad to see it go, and even called after it, but it was too late – the coats were too tightly packed for it to have squeezed between them. I could only presume that it had somehow dematerialised."

There are many types of devas – varying greatly both in power and in level of spiritual evolution. This little "brownie", as Alyson calls it, is clearly a world away from some of the awe-inspiringly beautiful devas illustrated by Ethelwynne M. Quail in Geoffrey Hodson's fascinating book, *The Kingdom of the Gods*.

Hinduism

There are many Gods in the age-old religion of Hinduism, although worship of them is not as highly esteemed as worship of Sri Krishna, according to the Hindu classic, the *Bhagavad Gita* (9.23-25).

The delivery of the *Bhagavad Gita* is one of the most unusual stories of Divine revelation I know of. The Lord Krishna is driving the chariot of a Prince named Arjuna on the battlefield. As he does so he delivers one of the most profound philosophies ever given to Earth.

Before combat begins, a sage named Veda Vyasa offers Arjuna's uncle, King Dhritarashtra, who was blind, the gift of sight so that he would be able to see what was going on. But, having no desire to witness the imminent slaughter of his family, he declined. However, he did want someone to tell him about it, so Veda Vyasa gave a man named Sanjaya, the King's counsellor and charioteer, the remarkable power of being able to see, hear, or in some other way become aware of every detail of the war, 24 hours a day, without ever feeling tired, and without any risk of injury. After ten days of fighting Sanjaya informs the King that Arjuna has defeated the warrior Bhishma. The King then asks Sanjaya to tell him the whole story, which he does.

Zoroastrianism

Little is known about Zoroaster (also known as Zarathustra, Zarathushtra, or Zartosht), founder of Zoroastrianism. Estimates of when he lived vary from hundreds to thousands of years BC. He was probably born in Northern Iran, and was interested in spiritual matters from a young age. When he was thirty he had a Divine vision of Ahura Mazda, the Lord, and subsequently communed with several holy immortals, or archangels, known as *ameshas spentas*.

His message was slow to win hearts among the people he preached to. However, a decade or so after his vision, a king named Vishtaspa, who ruled a kingdom in Central Asia, and his queen, Hutosa, were so impressed by his teaching that it ended up becoming their country's official religion.

The Judaeo-Christian tradition

In the Judaeo-Christian tradition, two individuals immediately spring to mind as having had what are probably two of the most common elements to Divine revelation – hearing a voice and seeing a vision of some kind.

We will never know if Moses had any inkling as he woke up that morning what was going to happen to him that fateful day. We can only imagine his alarm when, while out tending his father-in-law's flock, "the angel of the LORD appeared unto him in a flame of fire out of the midst of a bush" (Exodus 3.2). What's more, although the bush was burning, miraculously, it wasn't burnt.

The Lord spoke to Moses, and instructed him in his mission. Moses was naturally concerned that no one would believe that the Lord had appeared to him, so the Lord performed two miracles, illustrating his great power. Moses had a staff in his hand, which the Lord told him to throw on the ground. Moses obeyed and the staff turned into a snake. Understandably, Moses dashed away from it, but the Lord instructed him to "take it by the tail" (Exodus 4.4), which, showing great courage, again he obeyed. When he did so the snake turned back into a staff. The next miracle was to make Moses' hand seem "leprous" one moment, and normal again the next.

The Lord then said that if people didn't believe these things, then Moses could demonstrate a third kind of miracle: if he took water from the Nile and poured it on dry ground, it would turn to blood. Moses was still apprehensive, however, and explained his worry that he wasn't "eloquent" enough, and was "slow of speech" (Exodus 4.10), but the Lord was firm. He told him that he would help him and teach him what to say. But Moses still wasn't happy, and asked the Lord to send someone else to do it.

This didn't go down well with the Lord, but, either through compassion or exasperation, he suggested that Moses' brother Aaron could look after the public-speaking side of things, and promised that they would both receive Divine help.

One of the things that interests me most about this story is the name of the Lord, as revealed in Exodus 3.14: "And God said unto Moses, I AM THAT I AM: and he said, Thus shalt thou say unto the children of Israel, I AM hath sent me unto you." "I AM" is a mystical affirmation, and "I AM THAT I AM" is in fact the translation of a Sanskrit mantra.

Many thousands of words later, the Bible tells another story of someone blessed with Divine contact. This time, however, not only was the person themselves shocked – but so was everyone else; not so much at the miracle itself, but at who experienced it. If ever there was a story to inspire the worst of us – here it is. If ever there was proof, to believers at least, that no one is beyond redemption – then this is it. A far cry from the pietousness of Victorian churchianity, here is a miracle infinitely more shocking than water being turned into wine – here *bad* is being turned into *good*.

St Paul, or rather Saul of Tarsus, as he was formerly known, was a Jewish rabbi with Roman citizenship, who made a living from tent-making. Regarding Christianity as an outrageous affront to Pharisaic Judaism, a sect which focused on purity and adherence to the law of Moses, he became a keen enemy of the heretical new religion – evidently desiring nothing less than its total annihilation.

A position which was to change in the most dramatic way possible.

While on his way to Damascus, "suddenly there shined round about him a light from heaven" (Acts 9.3). He then "fell to the earth, and heard a voice saying unto him, Saul, Saul, why persecutest thou me?" (Acts 9.4). He asked who it was speaking, and the reply came: "I am Jesus whom thou persecutest" (Acts 9.5). "Trembling and astonished" he then asked what he would have him do – to which the reply came that he should go to the city and he'd find out there. His travelling companions were, as might be expected, "speechless" as a result of "hearing a voice, but seeing no man" (Acts 9.7).

He was blinded and neither ate nor drank for three days.

Meanwhile the Lord appeared in a dream to a Christian called Ananias and asked him to go to a house on Straight Street to find Saul of Tarsus, who, in a vision, had learnt that a man called Ananias would come and heal his blindness by placing his hands on him. Ananias was hesitant: he'd heard what kind of man Saul of Tarsus was, but the Lord was adamant, explaining that Saul had been chosen to spread the Gospel among Jews and non-Jews alike. So, being a faithful Christian, Ananias did as he was told.

Saul's sight duly recovered, he was baptised and – much to

everyone's amazement – he set about preaching the Gospel. These must have been testing times for the new convert: there were Jews who wanted him dead, and Christians who were afraid of him. Nevertheless, he managed to become one of the greatest champions of Christianity ever – being particularly significant in wishing to extend the Gospel to non-Jews, and in not requiring these non-Jewish converts to observe Jewish law, which many early Jewish Christians had continued to do, either in order to avoid persecution or simply because old habits die hard.

Islam

Several hundred years later, in about 570, The Prophet Muhammad was born in Mecca (Makkah in Arabic), in what is now Saudi Arabia. His father, a merchant, passed away before he was born, and when he was only six, his mother also died. He was looked after by his grandfather for a while but he died just two years later, after which he was cared for by his uncle.

After working as a shepherd, he worked as a merchant, and became popular for his honesty, fairness and good sense. He is also said to have been extremely handsome. There was a mole on his back between his shoulders, regarded by some as a sign of his destiny as a Prophet. At the age of around 25, he married a woman called Khadijah who was to become one of his first disciples.

One day when he was about 40, while he was meditating in a cave in the mountains outside the city, The Angel Gabriel (Jibril in Arabic) came to him and gave him a revelation which he was told to learn and repeat to other people. He continued to receive Divine revelations for the rest of his life.

Sikhism

Guru Nanak was born in 1469 in a village in Punjab to a middle-class family. His parents were Hindus, but he grew up among both Hindus and Muslims. He showed signs of his special destiny from an early age, including demonstrating his charitable nature by giving money to wandering holy men – much to the annoyance of his father who did not regard exchanging money for blessings in as positive a light as did his unusual son. Various miracles are attached to the story of his childhood, including one occasion when he was shaded from the sun by the hood of a cobra as he slept.

Jai Ram, husband of his devoted sister Nanaki, helped him get a job looking after the state granary. He would get up very early every morning, go to the river and meditate before work, but one morning he disappeared. His clothes were seen on the bank, but the man himself was nowhere to be found. The natural assumption was that he had drowned.

For three days he was submerged in water, during which time he experienced a Divine vision and received instructions in his mission. He quit his job and began a new life travelling around spreading the Divine message.

In the *Guru Granth Sahib* (the central text of Sikhism which is revered as much as a living Guru), he states that he only said what the Lord commanded him to say – that as he received the Divine Word (known as *Gurbani*) from the Lord, he imparted it to others. (Wadhans Mohalla 1, p-566; Tilang Mohalla 1, p-722). He would sing as he was blessed with the Divine Word, while his companion Mardana, played an instrument called a *rabab*, which resembles a guitar.

Buddhism

Few people realise how significant a role mediumship – albeit of an unusual kind – plays in Buddhism. Even today, according to his autobiography, *Freedom in Exile*, the Dalai Lama, head of the Gelukpa, or Yellow Hat, order of Tibetan Buddhists, consults an oracle known as "Nechung". This is not just for the sake of tradition. Although he makes it clear that he is not *dependent* on the advice he receives from Nechung – that he has other, less paranormal sources of advice as well – he does go as far as to say that he has never known the oracle to be wrong.

The medium, known as the *"kuten"*, wears a costume which is so heavy that prior to going into trance he has trouble walking normally. When the intelligence, Dorje Drakden, a deity responsible for protecting the Dalai Lama, has fully taken over the *kuten's* body, he is able to move with great energy, apparently oblivious to the mass of his attire.

Ancient Greece

That Greek mythology has proved to be such fertile soil for the growth and blossoming of Western art is perhaps its greatest legacy to the post-ancient world – from paintings like Botticelli's *Birth of Venus* to musical works like Offenbach's operetta *Orpheus in the Underworld*, from sculptures like Bernini's *Apollo and Daphne*, to plays like Racine's *Phèdre*. In more recent years even Disney has been inspired by the timeless appeal of the story of the hero Hercules – albeit in a very modern form.

No one really knows where the Greek myths originate from – some are perhaps mystical or philosophical allegories, others could be exaggerated accounts of things that really happened. People don't believe in their literal truth any more, but it seems that they were taken seriously by the general populace of Ancient Greece, however outlandish, unspiritual and amoral some of them may seem to us now. It is interesting to note that the philosopher Plato was extremely radical in claiming that God and the Gods were all *good* – an assertion which would have been considered naïve, and gravely contradicted the wild tales of the Gods' villainous behaviour – including violence, incest and rape – not to mention their fiery, untamed emotions.

Certain Gods could be contacted via an oracle, the most famous of which is probably the Oracle at Delphi, which was a vehicle for the wisdom of the God Apollo. The medium would be a local woman, over fifty, who was known as the "Pythia", who would live separated from her husband and wear the clothes of a young girl, reflecting the fact that the role had, in a bygone age, been filled by someone younger. The importance of her role should not be underestimated. Far from being the "Mystic Meg" of the ancient world, her advice was evidently treated with great respect, and was sought regarding subjects of genuine importance such as politics or war. In addition, consultation with the oracle was never an informal chitchat, on the contrary, it was a highly ritualised undertaking requiring various preparations.

The Pythia would wash in the Castalian spring and then drink from Cassotis, another sacred spring, before going into her underground chamber in the temple, where she would sit on a kind of sacred tripod and chew laurel leaves, which were associated with Apollo. Only then could she begin.

Many centuries later, in 1503, in St Rémy de Provence, France, a boy called Michel was born to an ordinary Jewish family (who at some point converted to Roman Catholicism) – a boy who was to grow up to become one of the most famous seers of all time. He practised a method of divination which had been used at the Ancient Greek Oracle of Branchus, where Apollo had also been identified as the source of the prophecy, just as he had at Delphi.

Nothing with Nostradamus is entirely straightforward, but what we appear to have in his first two quatrains is a description of a method, which resulted in the ability to prophesy using both vision and hearing – presumably in their psychic aspects.

Picture the scene. It is night time. A man sits alone – in secret – practising a mysterious ancient technique. He places a bowl of water atop a brass tripod. He becomes aware of a flame. In his hand is a wand. He wets the hem of his robe and his foot. There's a voice. He trembles. Finally *"Le divin pres s'assied"* – the divinity sits near.

* * *

Apollo, as well as being a source of prophecy and guidance, was also associated with, among many other things, music. Some believed that he incarnated upon earth as Pythagoras, who is usually associated with mathematics, but was also a remarkable mystic and musician.

Indeed Pythagoras and Apollo had much in common. He played the lyre, which was Apollo's chosen instrument, and more remarkably could hear the music of the cosmos, a feat beyond the capabilities of his students and more in-keeping with what one would expect from a God than a mortal. He used music (which could be heard by others) not just to arouse psychic awareness, but also to heal people physically and mentally, thus bridging the usually unbridgeable divide between Gods and mortals yet further, added to which Apollo was associated with healing. He set up his academy at Croton (now Crotone in Southern Italy) – a town which according to legend had been founded by a man named Myskellos on the instructions of Apollo which had been given through the Pythia. But most incredibly of all, he purportedly had a "golden thigh" – gold being associated with Apollo. The exact nature of the golden thigh remains mysterious, though it has been mooted that it was a birthmark.

Pythagoras believed that the planets of the solar system were inhabited by beings spiritually superior to us – and that the whole universe was full of intelligences of varying degrees of physicality, who sometimes acted as guides for humanity. Two "people" (or Gods?) who showed distinct signs of otherworldliness who Pythagoras is reported to have come into contact with were Astraios, his adopted brother, and Abaris, the Hyperborean.

Astraios was discovered by Pythagoras's father, Mnesarchus, who one day came across the parentless infant while travelling. The child was miraculous in that he was living off dew, and was able gaze at the sun without blinking. Mnesarchus adopted him and gave him his name, which means "starry".

Abaris was a priest of Apollo who may have taught Pythagoras. He is identified as a "Hyperborean", the term "Hyperborean" referring to a place in the far north resembling paradise, peopled by a race of beings who were both joyous and spiritually-minded. He never ate; apparently helped save the people of Sparta from plagues; and travelled on a flying "arrow", which may also have been used by Pythagoras. The exact nature of the "arrow" remains tantalisingly elusive – as indeed does the true nature of Pythagoras, his genius and his magic.

* * *

Dr King had always said that the word "Aetherius" derived from Greek, so as a member of The Aetherius Society, I was particularly interested to discover in Hesiod's *Theogony* (a work about Greek mythology dating back to around 700 BC) the existence of a Greek God called Aether.

Which brings me onto the chapter in which I share my own dearly-held spiritual beliefs...

CHAPTER 12

Space

"The Love which moves the sun and the other stars"
Dante Alighieri

One sunny Saturday morning in May 1954 a young Englishman, while drying dishes in his small flat in Maida Vale, London, heard a very unusual voice – with a yet more unusual command:

"Prepare yourself! You are to become the voice of Interplanetary Parliament."

He tells us that it came from outside of himself and struck his ear drums "with a somewhat gentle firmness", but he confesses to being unable to describe the "tonal qualities" of this "alien sound". He also describes the suddenness of it as it came into his mind as "numbing".

Even though the young man, a bachelor in his mid-thirties, had never even heard of "Interplanetary Parliament", he knew the experience wasn't his imagination; he was already far too skilled a medium to make a silly mistake like that. He had been practising advanced forms of yoga intensely for many years, and had developed remarkable powers of concentration and detachment. He was way beyond the psychic stage that people like me are at. Nevertheless he describes feeling "turmoil", "bewilderment" and "hopeless frustration" – presumably at the lack of any explanation to accompany the experience. He also says he felt such "terrible loneliness" that he would "almost weep" when he returned at night to the tiny room in which it had happened – strong words indeed for a yogi of his calibre.

This apparently ordinary young man knew without doubt that something extraordinary had happened – and he knew that whatever it was, it was very important.

An unenviable situation on the face of it – and yet one which would turn out to be so hugely significant that it would change the world.

* * *

This, to me, is the most important chapter of this book. And, although the vast majority of it is the result of someone else's wisdom rather than my own direct experience, it is also the chapter that I like the best. Not because it is the best written, or the easiest to believe – but because it means the most to me.

I have been Executive Secretary of The Aetherius Society in Europe for over 25 years and this chapter is about the beliefs of The Aetherius Society. My own channelled communications with higher realms are not an official part of the beliefs of The Aetherius Society – they are my own experiences which I offer to anyone inside or outside The Aetherius Society to believe, disbelieve, or just be open-minded about.

What you are about to read is an overview of the most elevated teachings I have ever come across.

* * *

For countless centuries the Gods have watched over our world with a sadness deeper than any sadness ever known to any mortal – and with a love greater than any love ever known to any mortal.

They have sent their emissaries at different times, to different places, with different messages to help suffering humanity in different ways. Jesus, Krishna, Buddha, Confucius, Lao Zi – these are just some of the courageous and selfless beings who have volunteered to live among us in this strange and savage world we have created for ourselves. They have willingly quit the supra-heavenly spheres which are the natural dwelling places of the Gods and chosen to suffer the confines of terrestrial flesh, with dulled terrestrial senses, and profoundly limited terrestrial minds – in order to teach us how to pull ourselves out of our ignorance and, as a result, be able to enjoy the same bliss that they enjoy.

But instead of welcoming such teachers with open arms, we have, on the whole, either ignored them, ridiculed them, or even killed them – or all three. A few have tried to follow their teachings, and to spread their message of hope – but not many. It's only after the teachings have gone through a process of "refinement" that they become palatable to the stubborn mass of humanity. It's like turning healthy sugar cane into sickly icing sugar, losing almost every vestige of its original nutritional value in the process. In some cases, the process has not even been so-called "refinement", but downright poisoning. You need look no further than the Spanish Inquisition or terrorism carried out in the name of various religions to see this.

We live in exciting times, which is both a blessing and a curse. It is common knowledge that we have enough weaponry to cause untold carnage, suffering and devastation. We have reached a point in our history now where it's either make or break. Seeing this, the Gods have flung the door to the secrets of the Cosmos wide open – in the fervent hope that we will use this knowledge to build ourselves a better world.

* * *

Just as there are planes which exist at different frequencies of vibration on Earth, to which we go between incarnations, there are also different frequencies on other planets. This is an amazing thought because it puts the question of extraterrestrial life in a whole new light. Planets which to our limited science seem to be nothing more than barren lumps of rock, on a different frequency could be teeming with life of many kinds. Whole alien civilisations could exist for millennia while remaining completely invisible to us. We could send astronauts to a planet for a decade – researching, studying, mapping, investigating – and they could return to Earth totally unaware of the life which existed there. It would be like going to someone's house and only looking for them downstairs, when in fact they lived on the second floor, and then concluding the house was empty.

Mainstream science is starting to look at concepts that were formerly the province of metaphysics. Scientists have recently started to accept that we are not alone in the universe. The idea that our nearest neighbours – Mars, Venus and the other planets in our Solar System – might house life cloaked to our physical senses, is not as outrageous as it used to be. I was once on the radio doing an interview about extraterrestrial life with Professor Martin Rees, a prominent British cosmologist and astrophysicist who holds the title of Astronomer Royal. When asked, he did agree that science should no longer dismiss the possibility of life not-as-we-know-it right on our own doorstep, in this very Solar System.

How times have changed. Where might science take us in the next fifty years? With concepts like parallel universes and a multi-dimensional cosmos, is it feasible that sufficient evidence might be found to convince even the most hardened cynic that life can exist in a higher form than our own?

I'm sure this will happen one day – and the sooner the better.

The existence of life on other planets – even close ones – now not quite so far-fetched, the question arises: if they do exist, but we can't contact them, why don't they contact us. Is it because they, like us, are unaware of our existence? Is it because they harbour a sinister plan to attack us? Or is it because they are just not interested?

No, no, and no.

The fact is that they *have* contacted us, many times – they just haven't done it in the way that people may have been expecting them to. But they are alien, so the fact that they should do things in an alien way should hardly come as a great shock to us. Often they may not even have revealed where they came from – humanity not being sufficiently awake to understand such a revelation.

But times have changed – and now, awake or not, the truth is out.

* * *

The unusual happening which occurred on May 8th, 1954, in Maida Vale, meant that George King's life would never be the same again.

It wasn't until eight days afterwards that he decided to do the most obvious thing of all to a yogi – meditate upon what had happened – true meditation being the key to true knowledge.

He didn't have to wait long. Astonishingly, a man in white robes walked *through* the locked door to the room – without opening it, or damaging it in any way. Nevertheless, he seemed "real enough"; the floorboards creaked as he walked, as did the old chair he sat himself down in.

The young yogi immediately recognised the great Swami before him – a spiritual teacher alive at that time in a "somewhat rotund physical body" in the Himalayas – but has never publicly revealed his name.

The uninvited, but only too welcome, visitor gave him the explanation he had been seeking, and instructed him in certain spiritual practices. He was also told that helpers would be brought into his orbit, and that he would get a letter from a school of yoga in London, which he should attend for a few months, assiduously practising the exercises taught there. The Swami then departed in the same way he had arrived – walking straight through the locked door.

This was to set the stage for a very unexpected change of direction in George King's life. Destined to be more than just a yogi-medium capable of contacting discarnates on the higher realms, it wasn't long before he was in regular communication with Gods from other worlds, or "Cosmic Masters", as they have come to be known.

The voice he had heard that fateful day turned out to be that of a Cosmic Master from the higher spheres of Venus, known by the pseudonym "Aetherius" – hence the name of the organisation Dr King founded the following year: The Aetherius Society.

According to Aetherius Society philosophy, the Gods – or Avatars – who have come to Earth to help us help ourselves, are not "spirit beings" from a nebulous heaven – they are members of extremely advanced extraterrestrial civilisations which exist on the higher spheres of other planets in this Solar System. For example,

The Master Jesus and The Lord Buddha were from Venus, St Peter was from Mars, Sri Krishna was from Saturn. This may sound strange, but this is only because we are used to thinking in a certain way. In fact, the assertion that The Master Jesus, for example, was one of several Cosmic Masters who incarnated on Earth is a far more plausible belief than to declare that he was the one and only Son of God.

Like Ascended Masters, Cosmic Masters do not need to go through reincarnation; they are not born as children, and they do not die in the way that we do. But unlike Ascended Masters, who live on Earth, they have the benefit of the highly elevated experience cycles which exist on their planets. Ascended Masters do visit other planets, and Cosmic Masters do come here, but generally speaking Ascended Masters live on Earth, and Cosmic Masters live on other planets.

We cannot even begin to imagine what it must have been like for a great Cosmic Master like Jesus to sacrifice the bliss of life on Venus to come to Earth and mix with ordinary people. There's probably a lot more difference between a Cosmic Master and someone like you and me, than there is between someone like you and me and a rat, for example. Would you volunteer to leave everything you knew and loved behind in order to be born as a baby rat because a particular group of rats needed your help?

Even Cosmic Masters like The Lord Babaji, who is from Saturn, who reside on Earth without suffering the limitation of having been born into a mortal terrestrial body, are making a sacrifice so great as to be far beyond our comprehension.

Why is such sacrifice necessary you may ask. If they are so advanced why don't they just fly here?

Well, sometimes they do.

* * *

The UFO phenomenon is nothing new. Mysterious aerial objects have been sighted for millennia. The concept of a "vimana" – translated as "flying celestial vehicle" in the ancient Hindu *Ramayana* is very similar to our idea of a spacecraft, as are the numerous celestial objects reported in the Bible, described by words such as "cloud" (Ezekiel 1.4), "flying scroll" (Zechariah 5.1-2), or "chariot of fire" (2 Kings 2.11). These words may strike us as inadequate names for such an amazing thing as an interplanetary spacecraft, and of course they are, but when compared with "flying saucer" or "cigar-shaped object" they seem comparatively sophisticated. Arguably the most remarkable account of all in the Bible of a UFO is the Star of Bethlehem (Matthew 2.9-10) – which could not possibly have been a star: stars do not move and then stand still over where a baby is.

In more recent times, there have been countless sightings of mysterious aerial phenomena. Many of these can be explained away easily, or hang on the word of one solitary unreliable witness. But many cannot and do not. There are books on UFOs listing case after case of highly credible people, such as pilots or military personnel, seeing inexplicable lights in the sky. Sometimes people even report landings. An incident which particularly caught my attention was the well-witnessed purported landing of an alien craft in a park in the Russian city of Voronezh. On this occasion it wasn't just the craft that was seen, but a tall alien, and a something like a robot, as well.

It should be noted that not all close encounters with extraterrestrials are all that they seem – even though they may be genuine paranormal experiences. The more sinister cases, including encounters with extremely unpleasant intelligences, are not the result of alien activity at all; they are the result of lower astral interference (discussed in its basic form in Chapter 6) of a particularly malevolent nature. There are in the lower astral realms, as you can imagine, discarnates who wish to do all they can to convince people that extraterrestrials are not to be trusted, in order to deflect attention away from the spiritual message of the Cosmic Masters.

UFOs are still being seen – but sightings seem to have dwindled in the last few years. Perhaps unsurprisingly, the people who worked closely with Dr King saw them many times; in fact it sometimes seemed as though they were following him around! I had several sightings during his lifetime, but have only had one since his passing.

Until today that was. On the very evening I wrote this paragraph Alyson and I saw an unmistakable UFO near our home in southwest London. Alyson saw it first – unaware what I had written that day. It was moving in a wide arc across the night sky – faster than a plane, and without the flashing lights that planes have. It seemed to be lower in the sky than the stars and wasn't moving like a meteorite or a satellite. Another example of synchronicity?

My first sighting took place when I was a student at Hull University. I had recently been introduced to The Aetherius Society by my very close friend Dr John Holder, who was doing his PhD in biochemistry at the time, and I was wondering whether or not to buy some Aetherius Society books and tapes. I wanted them very much, but I had very little money, and I also needed some new gym shoes. After prevaricating for some time I decided to go without the gym shoes and get the books and tapes.

A few days later, John saw a UFO in the area, which he had seen from the postgraduates' common room window. He drove home and told me, and, in great excitement, the two of us drove off in our battered old Austin A55 to get a better look at the "cigar-shaped object".

It was quite low – lower than the moon or the stars – moving very slowly, brightly illuminated in the night sky.

We parked the car, climbed over a tall fence and walked across the damp field to get a better look, but it became obscured by a large oak tree. I happened to glance down.

Under the oak tree was – a brand new pair of gym shoes.

There was nothing extraordinary about them. They were an ordinary brand. They hadn't been manufactured on the moon or anything like that. In fact I don't even believe that the UFO had anything to do with their being there. It was the synchronicity that struck me, nothing else. Of all things to find – and of all times to find them – gym shoes under an oak tree couldn't have been a better sign as far as I was concerned. Here was a literal example of the principle of "what you reject is laid at your feet" right before my eyes.

A small thing – yes. But for me a significant one.

Since that time, I have been amazed, not just at subsequent sightings I have been fortunate enough to have, but at the timing of other people's sightings. Once I was on a radio call-in show with a well-known radio DJ doing an interview on UFOs, during which this DJ said, addressing extraterrestrials, words to the effect of "Well if you're out there, show yourselves!"

Shortly afterwards we had a call from a man who had been listening to the show with his wife and family as they were driving along in the west country. He said a UFO had come into view and radiated a beam of light onto their car bonnet, apparently rendering the car immobile. The story even reached the London paper *The Evening Standard*, though the man and his family were unwilling to take the publicity any further.

In 1996 when I was involved in a tour around the UK promoting the truth about UFOs, there were two remarkable sightings reported. The tour, which consisted of 22 cities, began in Leicester and ended in Torquay. About an hour before the Leicester lecture was about to start, there was a UFO sighting in Leicester by people who knew nothing about the lecture. And, at the end of the tour, the day I arrived in Torquay, I picked up a local newspaper and saw a story on its front page saying a UFO had been seen heading that way!

* * *

Regardless of how many sightings there are, however, the simple fact remains that extraterrestrials have not landed and publicly presented themselves for all the world to see. Such a thing will one day happen – but when, depends on us.

The reason it hasn't happened yet is *Karma*, discussed in Chapter 1. Consider your own karmic pattern. What percentage of your life is devoted to spiritual work? What percentage of your energy is expended on selfish pursuits? How much control do you have over your basic emotions? How long do you spend in meditation every day? Chances are that you are more spiritual than most people on the planet, or you wouldn't be reading this book – but even the best of us leave a lot to be desired in terms of how advanced we *could* be if we really took to the spiritual path full-on.

Now think of the rest of the world – much of which has no interest in spirituality whatsoever. In fact a good portion of the world is actively opposed to spirituality of any kind – look at the number of dictatorships and corrupt governments there are in the world. Look at the warmongering and murder which take place every single day. Look at the evil which goes on in the name of religion.

If you weigh up the good against the bad – the balance is far from impressive.

And we are all responsible for world karma.

This means that the karmic pattern of humanity as a whole is not good. In the simplest possible terms: we don't deserve the full and open support of the Cosmic Masters – or the Ascended Masters for that matter. It's not that they don't want to help – they're not watching us, going "Tut, tut, they'll have to do better than that before we can be bothered to do anything for that lot of scoundrels!" Quite the reverse. They would love nothing more than to directly intervene in world affairs and give us the full benefit of their advanced science and high level of culture, so that we could live like they live.

But the very reason they have such an advanced science and high level of culture is because they work in perfect harmony with the Law of Karma – the law which prevents them from such direct intervention.

Again, it's important to stress that Karma isn't out to get us. It's not malevolent in any sense. It's a natural law, a thread running through the whole fabric of creation, which serves to teach us, through experience, how to evolve towards the state of God-consciousness which is our destiny. Compare the relationship we have with the Cosmic Masters with that of a child and parent – a parent who wants the best for their child. Such a parent might help a little with their child's homework, but wouldn't dream of doing the child's homework for them – the child would learn nothing, and more than likely become arrogant and lazy as well. Likewise, if the Cosmic Masters landed publicly and sorted out all the problems on Earth, it would in fact, paradoxical though it may sound, do us more harm than good, because it would prevent us from learning the lessons we needed to learn. We would become even more decadent a race than we are today – and no doubt accrue yet more bad karma from our lack of appreciation of their efforts on our behalf.

Given the dire state of the world, it is remarkable that the Cosmic Masters have managed to do as much as they have for us. In their all-knowing compassion, they have found clever ways of working with what little good karma we have to offer and somehow manage to give us a fantastic amount of help. One of these ways is to be born as one of us. If a Cosmic Master suffers the same limitation of a terrestrial body that we suffer, they are, from a karmic point of view, less limited in their ability to help us. The idea that great Gods choose to suffer in this way for our benefit, because of our bad karma, is not a pleasant one – but it should be sufficiently stirring to inspire us to do the best we possibly can by these beings.

The more we cooperate with them, by heeding their teachings, the better our karmic pattern becomes, and, consequently, the more they are able to help us. For every step we take towards them, they take two towards us. In this way, we can create a spiral of positive karma which will cause the whole of humanity to evolve in the way that it should.

* * *

Another way they have found of helping us is by using someone on Earth, in a terrestrial body, as a medium for their teachings.

Dr King is certainly not the only medium in history to have had contact with extraterrestrials. The Swedish scientist, philosopher and mystic Emanuel Swedenborg (1688-1772) wrote a book called *Earths in the Universe*, published anonymously, possibly to avoid controversy, which related information he had gleaned from communicating with the inhabitants of other planets in this Solar System. I do not agree with all the material in the book, but I think it is impressive that anyone living at that time would even conceive of the possibility of communicating with spiritual intelligences on other planets. He was undoubtedly a highly inspired, evolved soul who may not have been a completely accurate medium, but was way ahead of his time.

There are also without doubt numerous false claims. As with assessing claims of contact with Ascended Masters, the best way to tell the true from the false is by the old biblical adage *"Ye shall know them by their fruits"* (Matthew 7.16). Use your common sense. I know someone who went to a small UFO convention once where they were proudly shown the "channelled" message of a being supposedly from the Pleiades. It consisted of nothing more than unintelligible "writing" and an infantile picture of a stereotypical cartoon alien with a banal caption. Even if such a message were genuine, what would be the point of it?

Likewise I once met a woman claiming contact with an

intelligence from Jupiter. When I asked her what kind of stuff she was getting from this Jupiterean, she told me that it was mainly agricultural in nature. I asked her if she had managed to put any of this agricultural information into practice: "Oh, no! We don't do any farming. We don't even really understand most of it."

Such people are of course either just making it up, deluded, or being made a fool of by some mischievous lower astral entity, in the same way that there are people who claim they are in touch with an Ascended Master when they aren't (see Chapter 10). This, combined with the cases of people being tricked into believing they have had an unpleasant, traumatic encounter with an alien, mentioned earlier, all serves to misinform the public about the true spiritual message of these great beings.

But even among those who have had genuine contacts, Dr King is remarkable in having publicly sustained his contact for over forty years – demonstrating a remarkable consistency of both content and tone – and in having been the channel for such a huge volume of information.

The information was received, generally, in one of two ways – in "Mental Transmissions" and "Cosmic Transmissions". Both involved the reception of *thought impulses*. Dr King explained that the difference between the two was that while receiving a Mental Transmission he would not have been able to say out loud the entire communication exactly as it was received, whereas, during the reception of a Cosmic Transmission the thought impulses could be translated into sound or speech, and therefore be shared with others in a way that was much more direct – indeed the majority of the Cosmic Transmissions, which number over 600, have been recorded on tape and preserved for posterity so they can be enjoyed in perpetuity.

Seeing him receiving a Mental Transmission, he made it look quite easy, though he did once comment that it was far more difficult than taking a phone call! He would remain conscious, and was able to reply to whatever the communicator was saying. Cosmic Transmissions, however, were delivered through him while he was in a deep, positive trance condition, called *samadhi*, which would have required the Kundalini to be raised to one of the higher chakras (see Chapters 2 and 10 for more information on trance and Kundalini respectively). It was in this state that the majority of The Aetherius Society's key teachings were given.

I remember once being with Dr King, in the sitting-room of his modest bungalow in Santa Barbara, when he was in rapport with a certain Cosmic Master. He was in quite frail health at the time, but something about the contact made him extremely vibrant, dynamic and energetic. Before he began his discussion with the Cosmic Master, he told him that I was also present describing me as his Secretary from London, and giving my name. As soon as he did so I felt a beautiful, tangible burst of love energy. It was a wonderful feeling, and I feel deeply privileged to have had such an experience. It was as though this was the way the Cosmic Master was greeting me. I didn't see anything, or hear anything, but the feeling was more than adequate to prove his presence to me – not that I needed proof since I had already known Dr King for many years. Although the energy was of a very high calibre, I have no doubt that a Master of such an elevated status would have made sure that the energy sent to me was *low* enough for me – had it been of an even higher calibre, which such a Master would definitely be capable of, either I wouldn't have felt it, or it would have been too powerful for me to handle.

* * *

You may be wondering – why him? Of all the billions of people on the planet, why was George King chosen for such an important task? This is a big question with many answers, but in this book I shall concentrate on just one – which is certainly one of the most important – and that is his qualifications as a yogi.

He had already been practising an average of 8-10 hours of yoga a day for about a decade when The Aetherius Society was founded. He was an expert in the advanced forms of many yogas – including Jnana Yoga, Raja Yoga, Bhakti Yoga, Mantra Yoga, Mudra Yoga and Kundalini Yoga. Not only had this enabled him to develop exceptional abilities as a medium, but it also made him a very reliable vehicle for information – a safe pair of hands if you like. Someone with the level of self-control that intense yoga practice teaches, would also have the strength of character to carry out the instructions of the Cosmic Masters – come what may – with an iron faith born from the realisation of how great these beings really are.

Some readers may envy Dr King his contact, if they believe it, but it should be pointed out that his life was far from easy. He was effectively on call 24 hours a day from May 1954 onwards. He lived modestly and worked long hours, very seldom taking any holiday – and even when he did he would still use the time to think about work. His message was extremely controversial – especially in the all-too-conservative 1950s – even resulting in his life being threatened. He was mercilessly ridiculed by a cynical press – despite the fact that he so manifestly had nothing to gain from his claims.

Few would have lasted the course – especially when a slight change of direction could have made his life so much easier.

It is hard to believe now just how controversial and outrageous his claims seemed in those days. I remember even as recently as the 1980s broadcasting on radio phone-ins when views such as these were still regarded by some callers as mad, dangerous or heretical. Now people are far more open-minded and most questions and points are fair and reasonable in tone. In fact, I was listening to a phone-in on UFOs and the paranormal the other night while driving home. The guest on the show was an academic sceptic who was being grilled by an outraged public – one caller even asked her what had happened to her to make her this way. How things have changed!

If Dr King had been prepared to compromise on the truth, to present the public with a more appealing message, there is no question that he could have been a very popular teacher and made a fortune as a result. He often commented that honesty cost him a lot of money. But he never wavered for a moment in his determination to teach, and live, the message, as given through him, by the Cosmic Masters – a message which, although uncompromising, is extremely hopeful.

* * *

We are all Divine. Every one of us – however much it may appear to the contrary – is a Spark of God. All we have to do is realise this fact. If we did, our lives would change dramatically – and this world would quickly become like the higher spheres. By "realise", I don't mean "believe", or "understand", or even "have faith". I mean *realise* in the literal sense of the word: *make real*. As Truth unfolds in the consciousness of someone experiencing the higher states of meditation, what until that time has been no more than an idea, becomes a living reality. Unshakable knowledge of one's own Divinity – and of the Divinity of all things – is realised to an extent that most of us cannot yet fully conceive of.

It used to be the general trend of serious spiritual seekers – especially in the yoga tradition – to cut themselves off from society. They would go off and live in a cave up a mountain, and practise various spiritual techniques in the hope of gaining Enlightenment, or join an ashram or a monastery or something like that. They would spend all their time and exert all their efforts on advancing themselves towards God-knowledge. Then, theoretically at least, if they lasted the course, once they had gained the wisdom they were after, they would come back down the mountain and teach others how to experience what they had experienced.

However, we live in pivotal times. We are standing on the threshold of great spiritual change – and all the while the threat of nuclear war still hangs like a guillotine above our necks – to name but one of the dangers which face us.

Spiritual action is needed. And it's needed now.

The message of the Cosmic Masters, given through Dr King, is essentially one of service to others – regardless of how enlightened we may or may not be. Instead of working for the bliss of Enlightenment to the exclusion of all else, we should be working to help other people in whatever ways we can. If doing this means sacrificing our plans to lead a life of solitude and contemplation, then we should make that sacrifice. But by the Law of Karma, such sacrifice cannot go unrewarded. Dr King stated that "for every hour you give up a meditative state, in future lives you will spend maybe a hundred hours in the same state" – exemplifying the principle of "what you reject is laid at your feet".

This is Karma Yoga – the yoga of action. Traditionally the term "Karma Yoga" referred more to the way you acted, rather than what you actually did: it meant that you should do your duty, whatever that duty may be, but do it with complete detachment. This philosophy is explained best in the great *Bhagavad Gita*, in which the Avatar Sri Krishna is urging a prince named Arjuna to go to war – not to glorify bloodshed, but because it is his duty, in this instance, to fight. But in order to be successful Arjuna must act with total detachment – which is easier said than done – or else he would reap any negative karma his actions may accrue.

The "New Age" meaning of Karma Yoga is different in emphasis. It still includes the idea of doing one's duty with detachment, but it is much more pro-actively altruistic, in that it stresses the need to help others, which is our greatest duty of all. We should seek out the best possible way we can be of service to the world and then live by it to the very best of our ability.

Although this is a slower path to Enlightenment than was the traditional method of retiring to a cave and practising an intense course of self-development – it is also a much surer, safer one.

It does not preclude self-development altogether. In fact, on the contrary, a certain degree of spiritual practice and introspection is very important. Spiritual practice oils the wheels of spiritual motivation. Our motive should be as pure as possible, it should never be tainted by desire for reward of any kind. It should also be driven by enthusiasm. A sense of duty, though admirable, will not last without constant regeneration, fuelled by single-minded spiritual passion.

Service can take many forms – from helping out in a charity shop to lecturing on yoga philosophy, from composing inspirational music to feeding the homeless, from mopping hospital floors to rescuing injured animals, from giving healing to giving spiritual teaching. Everyone capable of reading this book is capable of some kind of service. It is service, and service alone, which will fill the spiritual void in our lives. That's not to say that all our problems will instantly disappear. We will still have worries and make mistakes. But our perspective will change and gradually we will become free of the problems which held us back before.

In The Aetherius Society we perform service in various ways – most of which involve what we call "spiritual energy", a power which is able to heal and inspire.

Spiritual energy is *prana* conditioned by love. The concept of *prana* is common to many philosophies around the world. It is similar – to varying degrees – for example to the Chinese concept of *qi* (also spelt *ch'i*), which in Japan is called *ki* (hence *reiki*), to the Melanesian belief in *mana*, and to the Ancient Greek idea of *pneuma*. In some Western writings it is called "the universal life force", which makes sense because that is exactly what it is. In fact Dr King went one step further, defining it in the three-word maxim "*Prana* is Life", to which can be added his more poetic description of it as "the life of the atom and the vitality of the most elevated inspiration of the highest saint". But more important than understanding the exact subtleties of what *prana* is, is learning how to work with it.

The world desperately needs spiritual energy. In fact, Dr King has said that the only energy crisis on Earth today is the *spiritual* energy crisis. When the spiritual energy crisis is solved, the world's problems will be at an end. It can be directed to anything – even an inanimate object. Blessing something – be it a book, a building, an item of clothing or whatever – imbues it with a certain type of spiritual energy. Plants, animals and people can all be healed by it – in mind and in body. And the good news is that healing is something anyone can learn to do.

But more important even than giving healing to individuals is giving healing to the whole world. Extraordinary though it may seem, we can make a difference to the world, right here and now, using incredibly simple techniques, which will not only help others, but also improve our own karmic pattern – and as a result the karma of the world as well. We can also direct our love to the great beings to whom we owe so much: the Cosmic Masters, and even mightier beings than these, such as the living, breathing Mother Earth, a Goddess who in holy sacrifice, allows us to gain experience upon her great back, and the Sun – itself a living God – giver of life throughout the Solar System.

This is something you can try for yourself very easily. Stand up, or sit with back straight, raise the hands so that they are roughly parallel to your neck. Have the palms facing outwards. Close the eyes, and visualise a scintillating white light coming down through the head, neck, shoulders, and arms. Visualise it also coming down into the chest area and out into the heart chakra, a few inches in front of the chest. Now see this energy flowing through you, out through the palms and the heart chakra as a wonderful, living energy. You can direct it to humanity as a whole, or to a region in crisis. Always make your visualisation entirely positive. If an area is, for example, devastated by war, detach from that – bathe it in healing white light and see it as it should be. You can do this silently, or say a prayer of your choice, as you do the visualisation.

This is prayer – as it should be. The word "prayer" isn't very fashionable these days, and frankly I'm not surprised, when you look at what most people think prayer is. Kneeling down, head bowed, hands clasped against the chest mumbling a few words is not an effective method of sending healing to the world or of expressing appreciation to the great ones. It's better than nothing, certainly, but why settle with that when you could be enjoying the thrill of allowing a wonderful beam of magnificent white light to flow through you, in a practical, dynamic expression of Real Love?

* * *

It was an unusual experience of "dynamic prayer", as Dr King termed it, which first brought me into The Aetherius Society. I attended a lecture by John Holder, in which he talked about yogic prayer, organised by the Buddhist and Vedanta Society at Hull University – in fact it was the first time I'd met John. Afterwards, when I got home, I thought I'd try out the simple technique that John had taught everyone. I made the target of my prayer a homeless man I had seen earlier in the day – praying for maybe five or ten minutes. As the energy flowed through my aura I felt an amazing tingling sensation all over my body. Afterwards I went to bed thinking the sensation would subside. But it didn't. I lay awake for hours wondering what was going on. By about 4am, I'd had enough; I decided to walk to the place where the organiser of the lecture lived – which was about four miles away. It turned out that he didn't know anything about dynamic prayer – he'd never tried it – all he could do was tell me how

I could get in touch with John, who the next day I found at the Biochemistry Department. We arranged a time to meet – and I fired him with questions. The answers were to change my life.

Dr King introduced dynamic prayer as a natural way of invoking energy and sending it out to bring about a positive result. Its likelihood of success is not dependent on the whim of an old man on a cloud, but on quantifiable variables such as the number of people praying, the length of time the prayer goes on, and the degree of intensity of feeling behind the prayer. You are not going to bring about world peace by doing a little visualisation for a couple of minutes. Rome wasn't built in a day, as the saying goes. But nevertheless every brick counts. Your two minutes could play a crucial role. Combined with the efforts of people around the world – of all faiths and none – who concentrate on their desire for peace and freedom for all, it could work miracles.

However the number of people praying for peace and freedom in an unselfish way, not for themselves or their family or friends, but for people they've never even met, is not as large as it should be. And of those good people who do make the effort, how many of them really put all their love and feeling into it? How does passion for creating world peace compare with passion for winning the World Cup? Which are more heartfelt: the cheers of the average football supporter or the prayers of the average church-goer? Added to which, people pray at different times, in different places; it is rare to have a large group of people assemble together to pray, for example, for the relief of suffering after an earthquake immediately after news of the earthquake reaches them.

Prayer alone is not enough of course, you'd still need aid workers to go into the field, you'd still need diplomats negotiating for peace, and you'd still need doctors and nurses to look after the injured. But, ideally, in addition to this, huge numbers of people would respond almost instantly to a world crisis by gathering together in prayer both to send healing to those who were suffering as a result of the crisis, and also to give inspiration and strength to the aid workers, diplomats, doctors and nurses, who would be able to work better as a result.

But we do not live in an ideal world. That's why Dr King devised a mission called Operation Prayer Power.

* * *

Working with the idea that "prayer" is in fact a way of invoking a real energy – every bit as real as an energy like electricity in fact – Dr King knew that it was possible to put this energy into a physical container. On a very small scale something like this is going on all the time. Every time you think a thought, you are in fact sending out a small amount of energy, which to some degree will make an impression on an object you are touching at the time. That's why a psychic skilled in psychometry (psychic touch) can touch your watch, for example – something you are in contact with for most of your waking life – tune in, and come up with quite a lot about you. They are accessing information which you yourself have put into the watch without even realising it. Certain materials lend themselves to psychometry more than others – a metal watch would be easier to psychometrise than a plastic one for example. This is because some materials are better than others at storing this kind of energy.

Using this same principle Dr King invented a "Spiritual Energy Battery", which is filled with certain metals and crystals in such a way as to store spiritual energy in the best possible manner. People gather together on a regular basis and chant sacred mantra, a particularly effective way of invoking spiritual energy, all the while directing the energy, through visualisation, to someone who is praying right in front of the Battery, with one palm over the Battery's aperture. The prayers used come from a work called *The Twelve Blessings* which was channelled through Dr King by The Master Jesus. Putting your heart and soul into this extremely dynamic, vibrant way of helping the world is phenomenally inspirational – especially for the people who pray at the Battery itself, since everyone else's energy is flowing through them, as well as their own.

When there is a world disaster of some kind, or a particularly key moment when a great deal of good can be done, such as an important peace talk, the energy in the Battery is released using a specially-designed apparatus, called a "Spiritual Energy Radiator". Once the decision has been made exactly where we would like the energy to go, a small number of highly experienced members of The Aetherius Society are able to perform a certain ritual through which they can communicate with the Cosmic Masters. Please note that this is a one-way communication system – we can contact them, but, unfortunately, we are not advanced enough to receive a reply from them. This is not something we have just decided to do, it is a formal arrangement which Dr King set up with the Cosmic Masters during his lifetime which has enabled us to continue this "Cosmic Mission", called "Operation Prayer Power", after his passing. I must say that as one of those privileged to perform this ritual, it is one of the most sacred experiences of my life.

This means that at a moment's notice, hundreds of hours of

spiritual energy can be directed in a short time to a specific area to bring about relief of suffering in a very efficient way – on many occasions the results of releasing prayer energy in this way have been remarkable (more details of which are in *Contacts with the Gods from Space* which I co-authored with Dr King).

* * *

A Spiritual Energy Radiator can also be used to send out energy from a Cosmic source. On the morning of April 25th, 1986, in a very ordinary hotel in Arizona, a very extraordinary thing was to happen. I was part of a team who were with Dr King to assist him with some important spiritual work he was going to be doing in the area. I was sitting in his hotel room ready to help him in whatever way was necessary. He asked me to set up a table with pen, paper and some water, which indicated to me that he was about to get a Mental Transmission. This was only to be expected in view of the work we were doing. He then proceeded to take the Mental Transmission from a Cosmic Master, writing it down as he received it, while I sat in attendance in case he should need anything.

The information which came through was of a very unexpected nature. He was told that the Spiritual Energy Radiator in Los Angeles, was to be turned on in half an hour's time, indicating that a world emergency was imminent – a classic example of channelling being used for something of phenomenal importance.

A few hours later, on the other side of the world, at 1.23am Moscow time, the worst nuclear reactor disaster in history was to take place – the infamous explosion at Chernobyl, which the Soviets did not admit to for three days.

In 2002 the Russian newspaper *Pravda* revealed that eyewitnesses saw a UFO hovering above the fourth power-generating unit – the one which was destroyed – for six hours from when the trouble began. Many believe that the UFO prevented the disaster from being even worse than it was. The explosion which occurred was a thermal blast. If a nuclear explosion had taken place, it is thought that half of Europe would have been wiped off the map.

* * *

Another example of what we now have at our disposal to help the world is the nineteen mountains which were charged with spiritual energy in a Mission carried out between 1958 and 1961 called "Operation Starlight".

Dr King was instructed by the Cosmic Masters to climb 18 mountains around the world. He had very little money and only a handful of helpers, but somehow he managed it. When he reached the summits, or a high point, of each mountain he was used as a channel for an initial charge of a special kind of spiritual energy, which was directed into the mountain making it holy. This means that now, anyone who climbs one of these mountains, and does some kind of spiritual practice, can access this power. You do not have to be a member of The Aetherius Society to do this – in fact you don't even have to know or believe that the mountain is holy. The power responds to your motive and actions – nothing else. I know from experience how wonderful it can be to do spiritual practices on a holy mountain – the feeling you get as the spiritual power rises up through you and flows out to the world can be truly breathtaking.

The mountains are as follows. You would be strongly

recommended to seek advice on the safety procedures you need to follow to climb some of these mountains, and to pick a suitable time of year.

British Isles
Holdstone Down, Devon, England
Brown Willy, Cornwall, England
Ben Hope, The Highlands, Scotland
Craig-An-Leth-Chain, Grampian, Scotland
The Old Man of Coniston, Cumbria, England
Pen-Y-Fan, Powys, Wales
Carnedd Llywelyn, Gwynedd, Wales
Kinderscout, Derbyshire, England
Yes Tor, Devon, England

USA
Mount Baldy, California
Mount Tallac, California
Mount Adams, New Hampshire
Castle Peak, Colorado

Australia
Mount Kosciusko, New South Wales
Mount Ramshead, New South Wales

New Zealand
Mount Wakefield, Southern Island

Africa

Mount Kilimanjaro, Tanzania

(Note: Dr King did not climb this mountain; it was charged by three Members of The Spiritual Hierarchy of Earth, without Dr King being present to act as a channel for the energy.)

Europe

Mount Madrigerfluh, Swiss Alps, Switzerland

Le Nid d'Aigle, Mont Blanc, France

* * *

Another amazing revelation made in the cosmic contacts of Dr King is the concept of a "Spiritual Push". During a Spiritual Push all spiritual actions, whether they relate to a holy mountain or not, are potentised by a factor of 3000 in terms of their karmic power.

This is a difficult concept to grasp, since it seems almost too good to be true. A spacecraft, known as "Satellite Number Three", under the direction of a Cosmic Master from Mars radiates a special type of spiritual energy which enhances the karmic power of all spiritual actions. This doesn't mean that if you give someone healing that they get better 3000 times more quickly, but it does mean that any spiritual action helps the overall karma of the world 3000 times more than it normally would. There are four Spiritual Pushes a year, on the following dates, from midnight to midnight GMT in each case. I and many others have felt a distinct difference in the energy before and during a Spiritual Push.

Spiritual Push No. 1   April 18th – May 23rd

Spiritual Push No. 2	July 5th – August 5th
Spiritual Push No. 3	September 3rd – October 9th
Spiritual Push No. 4	November 4th – December 10th

Again, you don't have to be a member of The Aetherius Society, or even believe in the existence of Satellite Number Three to take advantage of the energy being radiated to the world at this time: this is something that anyone can do – all you need is a truly unselfish motive. Every time someone gives money to a good cause, every time someone helps a blind person cross the road, every time a Christian prays for peace, every time a Hindu praises Brahma, every time a humanist campaigns for justice – provided they are doing it for the right reasons – their efforts will be vastly more powerful, from a karmic point of view, during a Spiritual Push.

So you can see that the contacts of Dr King were extremely practical, focusing more on what we can actually do to help the world than on theoretical beliefs.

* * *

That George King led a remarkable life is not in doubt – though many are of course sceptical of his claims.

To those who have really experienced the spiritual magic that he taught, there is no doubt that he was 100% genuine. Even among those people who worked closely with him for many years, but left The Aetherius Society to do other things, I cannot recall a single one who left because they stopped believing that he was genuine. And among people in general who leave The Aetherius Society, many come back. Once you taste something this good, it's hard not to want to come back for more.

I worked closely with him for over twenty years. Even when we were on different sides of the Atlantic, we would speak on the phone almost every day. There's certainly no question in my mind that he was everything he said he was – and more. Even now, a decade after his passing, I feel more and more appreciative of him. Sometimes I couldn't understand why he did things the way he did, and occasionally I didn't agree with him, but as the years go by I am coming to the realisation that he was right about pretty much everything – certainly everything important – a rare thing for anyone to feel about anyone.

* * *

I hope this book has succeeded, to a small degree, in illustrating how much influence contact with higher beings has on all our lives – whether we are aware of it or not. Politics, art, science, religion, philosophy – none of these areas would be what they are today without this contact. Indeed, everything we do and think, is in some way, affected by the presence in our world of Gods, guides and guardian angels.

AFTERWORD

"The voice so sweet, the words so fair,
As some soft chime had stroked the air"
Ben Jonson

It was over 25 years ago that I saw Pixie in that sitting-room in Perth. It seemed extraordinary then – now it is just so normal, prosaic even. Why shouldn't a friend who's died want to make their presence felt? And why shouldn't I be able to see and hear them when they do? And if I can do it, why can't others too?

But there is another voice I am increasingly aware of – a far more important voice to me than Pixie, or any other guardian angel or guide I have been privileged to encounter. It is what the Bible calls the "the still small voice", and Theosophy refers to as "the voice of the silence".

This is the voice which can become our inner guardian angel and guide – and ultimately our God. Because it is our link to the Divine Spark within us all. The more we listen to it and act upon it, the closer we come to our real Self, referred to in yoga philosophy as the I AM Presence.

Thousands of years ago the great yogi Sri Patanjali laid down the essential steps of Raja Yoga, the path to union with God through psychic and mental control. He outlined the powers (*siddhis*) you could obtain along the way, but stressed that these should never become your goal. The aim of Raja Yoga was the perfection of the individual and the attainment of Enlightenment.

None of the great yogis who have come since – Swami Vivekananda, Swami Sivananda, Paramahansa Yogananda or any other – have attempted to alter the central principles of Raja Yoga as laid down by Sri Patanjali. They have thrown new light upon them from their own profound experience – but they have not modified the essential stages every student of this great practice needs to go through.

One of these stages, which is often overlooked by psychic teachers nowadays is called in Sanskrit, *pratyahara*. This involves controlling the physical senses – Swami Sivananda describes it as the withdrawal of the senses from the objects. According to Patanjali, and all the other great yogis, this ability is crucial BEFORE you can safely obtain the powers. Too many teachers nowadays conveniently try to bypass this, which makes them popular, but in my view lacking. Because without this detachment, you can lose contact with your inner voice. Then, all too often, the powers start to use you instead of you using them, which is a dangerous place to be.

There are those teachers who frown on any powers being developed at all. It has not occurred to them that these powers can be used to perform great service to others. Healing, just to name one, is a wonderful power we can all attain and use to help people, animals and even plants.

But powers, as Sri Patanjali says, are not the goal. They are just signs which manifest along the path. A person who claims to be enlightened, and yet has obtained no powers on the way, is not. An enlightened person would have awakened their inner psychic and spiritual abilities in one way or another, controlled them and rejected them before having gone on to the higher stage of true Enlightenment.

Channelling could be described as one of the powers. It is not for everyone, but it can be a wonderful way to serve others. As you progress in channelling you move from guardian angels, to higher guides and then, if you are advanced enough (which I for one am not) even to the Gods.

Whether you channel or not, you can still benefit from the wisdom, teaching and inspiration brought by some of those who do. And you can develop your own psychic and spiritual abilities, perhaps in even more useful ways, and apply them in service to others knowing that you will be cooperating with higher forces.

And as you do so, please remember that there is something even more precious than any powers or abilities you may develop along the way.

It is silent.

It is still.

It is the voice within.

BOOK REFERENCES

A Treatise on Cosmic Fire by Alice Bailey, Lucis Publishing Company, 2nd paperback edition, 1977, USA

Autobiography of a Yogi by Paramahansa Yogananda, Self-Realisation Fellowship, 12th edition – 12th paperbound printing, 1993, USA

Contacts with the Gods from Space by George King, D.D., with Richard Lawrence, The Aetherius Society, 1st edition, 1996, USA

Earths in the Universe by Emanuel Swedenborg, The Swedenborg Society, 3rd edition 1894, reprinted 1970, UK

Freedom in Exile – the autobiography of the Dalai Lama of Tibet by the Dalai Lama, Hodder and Stoughton, 1st edition, 1990, UK

Initiation, Human and Solar by Alice Bailey, Lucis Press Ltd, paperback new edition, 1972, UK

Isis Unveiled by Helena Petrovna Blavatsky, Theosophical University Press, reprint, 1988, USA

Life of Apollonius by Philostratus, translated by C. P. Jones, edited, abridged and introduced by G. W. Bowersock, Penguin Books Ltd., 1st edition, 1970, UK

Light on the Path by Mabel Collins, The Theosophical Publishing

House Ltd., unnumbered edition printed in 1972, UK

Operation Earth Light – a glimpse into the world of the Ascended Masters by Brian C. Keneipp, 1st edition, The Aetherius Press, 2000, USA

Popular Lectures on Theosophy by Annie Besant, The Theosophist Office, 2nd edition, 1912, India

Realise Your Inner Potential, by George King, D.D., and Richard Lawrence, Aetherius Press, 2nd edition, 2004, UK

The Book of the Dead by E. A. Wallis Budge, Arkana (Penguin Books Ltd), Arkana edition, 1989, UK

The Kingdom of the Gods by Geoffrey Hodson, illustrated by Ethelwynne M. Quail, The Theosophical Publishing House, 6th edition, 1970, India

The Magic of Healing by Richard Lawrence, Mind Body Spirit Direct, 2nd edition, 2004

The Nine Freedoms by George King, D.D., The Aetherius Press, 3rd impression, 2001, USA

The Secret Doctrine by Helena Petrovna Blavatsky, Theosophical University Press, facsimile edition, 1999, USA

The Tibetan Book of the Dead compiled and edited by W. Y. Evans-

Wentz, Oxford University Press, 4th edition, 1960, USA

The Twelve Blessings by George King, D.D., The Aetherius Press, 6th impression, 2000, USA

You Too Can Heal by George King, D.D., The Aetherius Society, 1976, USA

Ancient Classics
Bhagavad Gita
Hesiod's *Theogony*
Homer's *Iliad*
Ramayana
Sri Guru Granth Sahib
The Holy Bible (King James Version)

For more information

For more information about spiritual development workshops and lectures in the UK, contact:

The Inner Potential Centre
36 Kelvedon Road
Fulham
London
SW6 5BW
UK

www.innerpotential.org

For further information on The Aetherius Society, if you are in the UK call 020 7736 4187; if you're in the USA call 1 800 800 1354; or visit www.aetherius.org

To find out about Richard Lawrence's upcoming events, visit www.richardlawrence.co.uk

If you are not based in the UK or USA get in touch via either of the telephone numbers, or any of the websites, above to find out what's going on in your area.

INDEX

Oxford 2, 106
Palaeolithic peoples 31
parachute 21, 73
Patanjali, Sri 130, 197-198
Pen-Y-Fan 193
Perth viii, 197
Perugians 85
Phèdre 160
Philostratus 129
Piacenza 71
Pixie viii-x, 2, 18, 21, 197
plane (after-death realm) *see also* level, realm 7, 11, 121-122, 124-127, 168
Plato 161
pneuma 185
Poitiers 81
politics 30, 68, 88, 93, 161, 196
poltergeist 54
Popular Lectures on Theosophy 93
possession (by a discarnate) 34, 43, 64-66
Powys 193
prana 72, 185
pratyahara 198
Pravda 192
prayer 34, 58, 79, 83-84, 86, 120, 187-191, 195
Pretoria 88
Provence 85, 161
psychic 14-24, 28-30, 33, 37, 39-40, 42-45, 48-51, 57-59, 63, 69-70, 72, 88, 93, 95-97, 103, 129-131, 138, 144, 149, 162, 165, 189, 197-199
psychic centre *see* chakra
psychometry 189
Pythagoras 143, 162-163
Pythia 161, 163
qi 185
Quail, Ethelwynne M. 154

rabab 159
Rachmaninoff, Sergey 97
Racine 160
Raja Yoga 130, 181, 197-198
Rakoczy *see also* St Germain, Count 142
Ramakrishna, Sri 147
Ramayana 172
Ranikhet 139
Realise Your Inner Potential 43
realm (after-death realm) *see also* level, plane 3, 7-13, 18-19, 22, 29, 33, 35, 38, 41, 46-48, 52, 58-62, 64, 70, 73-74, 76, 89, 91-93, 95, 99-100, 102, 106, 113, 116, 119-120, 124, 127, 135, 137, 147, 166, 170, 173
rebirth *see also* reincarnation 32
Rees, Prof Martin 168
reiki 72, 185
Reims 80-81
reincarnation *see also* rebirth 13, 109, 132-133, 171
religion 34-35, 65, 67-68, 79, 82-83, 88, 91-93, 109, 116, 120, 147, 150-151, 154-155, 157, 167, 176, 196
Retreats (of The Spiritual Hierarchy of Earth) 148
Rivers State 35
Roman Catholicism 11, 63, 68, 79, 92, 102, 162
Rome 86-87, 128, 157, 188
Rosenkreuz, Christian 142
Rosicrucianism 142
Rosna, Charles B. 54
Rotorua 30-31
Royal Academy 97
Royal Air Force 21
Russia 91, 97, 142-143, 172, 192
St Catherine 79

Contacts with the Gods from Space

pathway to the new millennium

George King with Richard Lawrence

Read this amazing account with eyes wide and mouth open as you discover the fantastic truth about life on other planets, healing the world, the unknown history of the human race, and more – find the answers to the questions you never thought to ask! Whether you believe it or not – you are guaranteed a fascinating read. Includes excerpts of the remarkable communications channelled through the internationally acclaimed medium and spiritual teacher, Dr George King.

ISBN 0-937249-15-7; UK £9.99; US $14.95
Available from all good bookshops.

Here are some of the reviews it received when it was first published…

"…mind-blowing… makes for compulsive reading… The arguments are well balanced and the wealth of information is the backbone for the message being conveyed."
Encounters Magazine

"With an explosion of spiritually-angled publications… the time was clearly right for this accessible paperback."
Fortean Times

"The teachings explained in Contacts with the Gods from Space *answer many questions about humanity's origins, the role of ETs in our development… they also advocate the principle of spiritual ecology to assist us in creating a positive future…"*
Nexus Magazine

"…a well-written and well-documented book… bears a message we must hear over and over again…"
Whole Life Times

Available from The Inner Potential Centre, 36 Kelvedon Road, London, SW6 5BW, UK; tel 020 7736 4187; www.innerpotential.org
Please note that this book is not available from O Books' distributors.

Realise Your Inner Potential

a spiritual handbook for a new age
George King and Richard Lawrence

Realise Your Inner Potential is more than just a set of exercises – it is a manual for living. Read this book, adopt its practices and discover a new life of spiritual success and lasting fulfilment.

**Good Karma • Mantra • Healing • Personal Magnetism
Yoga Breathing • Psychic Powers • Inner Peace • Kundalini • Concentration
Mystic Visualisations • Intuition**

"Although 'personal development' has been the fastest-growing sector of British publishing over the last decade, few of its books are of lasting quality. One that should endure is Realise Your Inner Potential *by Dr George King and Richard Lawrence... King was one of the great spiritual teachers of the twentieth century..."* **Time Out**

ISBN 0-947550-03-8; UK £9.99 / ISBN 0-937249-16-5; US $19.95
Available from all good bookshops.

Realise Your Inner Potential - DVD
with Richard Lawrence

Fantastic both as a stand-alone guide, or as an accompaniment to the *Realise Your Inner Potential* book, this ground-breaking DVD teaches you key *Realise Your Inner Potential* techniques with a series of superb demonstrations, enhanced by CGI special effects.

Running Time: approx. 1 hour 25 minutes; UK £15.99; US $24.95

Realise Your Inner Potential - FREE CD
with Richard Lawrence

Get the book and DVD for the special price of just £19.99 and you will receive a free lecture CD!

**Available from The Inner Potential Centre, 36 Kelvedon Road, London, SW6 5BW, UK; tel 020 7736 4187; www.innerpotential.org
Please note that these items are not available from O Books' distributors.**